NEW ESSAYS ON THE RED BADGE OF COURAGE

★ The American Novel ★

GENERAL EDITOR

Emory Elliott, Princeton University

New Essays on
The Red Badge of Courage

Edited by

Lee Clark Mitchell

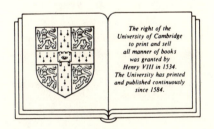

The right of the
University of Cambridge
to print and sell
all manner of books
was granted by
Henry VIII in 1534.
The University has printed
and published continuously
since 1584.

CAMBRIDGE UNIVERSITY PRESS

Cambridge

New York   New Rochelle

Melbourne   Sydney

Published by the Press Syndicate of the University of Cambridge
The Pitt Building, Trumpington Street, Cambridge CB2 1RP
32 East 57th Street, New York, NY 10022, USA
10 Stamford Road, Oakleigh, Melbourne 3166, Australia'

First published 1986
Reprinted 1988

Printed in the United States of America

Library of Congress Cataloging-in-Publication Data
New essays on The red badge of courage.
(The American novel)
Bibliography: p.
1. Crane, Stephen, 1871–1900. Red badge of courage.
I. Mitchell, Lee. II. Series.
PS1449.C85R397   1986   813'.4   86-9727

British Library Cataloguing in Publication Data
New essays on The red badge of courage.–
(The American novel)
1. Crane, Stephen. Red badge of courage
I. Mitchell, Lee.   II. Series.
813'.4   PS1449.C85R39

ISBN 0 521 30456 3 hard covers
ISBN 0 521 31512 3 paperback

Contents

v

Contents

Series Editor's Preface

In literary criticism the last twenty-five years have been particularly fruitful. Since the rise of the New Criticism in the 1950s, which focused attention of critics and readers upon the text itself – apart from history, biography, and society – there has emerged a wide variety of critical methods which have brought to literary works a rich diversity of perspectives: social, historical, political, psychological, economic, ideological, and philosophical. While attention to the text itself, as taught by the New Critics, remains at the core of contemporary interpretation, the widely shared assumption that works of art generate many different kinds of interpretation has opened up possibilities for new readings and new meanings.

Before this critical revolution, many American novels had come to be taken for granted by earlier generations of readers as having an established set of recognized interpretations. There was a sense among many students that the canon was established and that the larger thematic and interpretative issues had been decided. The task of the new reader was to examine the ways in which elements such as structure, style, and imagery contributed to each novel's acknowledged purpose. But recent criticism has brought these old assumptions into question and has thereby generated a wide variety of original, and often quite surprising, interpretations of the classics, as well as of rediscovered novels such as Kate Chopin's *The Awakening*, which has only recently entered the canon of works that scholars and critics study and that teachers assign their students.

The aim of The American Novel Series is to provide students of American literature and culture with introductory critical guides to

American novels now widely read and studied. Each volume is devoted to a single novel and begins with an introduction by the volume editor, a distinguished authority on the text. The introduction presents details of the novel's composition, publication history, and contemporary reception, as well as a survey of the major critical trends and readings from first publication to the present. This overview is followed by four or five original essays, specifically commissioned from senior scholars of established reputation and from outstanding younger critics. Each essay presents a distinct point of view, and together they constitute a forum of interpretative methods and of the best contemporary ideas on each text.

It is our hope that these volumes will convey the vitality of current critical work in American literature, generate new insights and excitement for students of the American novel, and inspire new respect for and new perspectives upon these major literary texts.

Emory Elliott
Princeton University

Note on the Text

The textual history of *The Red Badge of Courage* is obscure and complicated, and the following simply outlines issues detailed more fully in Hershel Parker's essay. Whether or not Crane started work on the novel in 1892, he had certainly begun writing by March 1893. After completing nearly one-third of a draft, he started over, this time (for lack of paper) writing on the unused sides of his first pages. By December 1893, he seems to have completed a novel of twenty-five chapters and some 55,000 words, and he spent nine months vainly trying to convince publishers to accept it. Finally, he took the manuscript to the Bachellor-Johnson news syndicate, which offered to serialize an abbreviated version of 18,000 words. The novel first appeared in this form in December 1894 in the New York *Press*, the Philadelphia *Press*, and hundreds of other papers throughout the country.

That same month, Crane received an acceptance from D. Appleton and Company, and a version 5,000 words shorter than the original manuscript was published in October 1895. Long since lost have been the typescripts used by both Bachellor and Appleton as fair copy for typesetting. Still extant, however, at the University of Virginia is a bound manuscript of 176 pages that is marked by various hands with emendations and cuts. Five pages from the original have been lost or destroyed, and four of six pages that constituted the original Chapter 12 are preserved in special collections at Harvard, Columbia, and the New York Public Library.

The major and continuing problems with establishing a reliable text begin with the manuscript, particularly since the reasons Crane had for cutting material remain unclear. Alterations suggested by Hamlin Garland, who was among the first to read the manuscript, have recently been called into question. And other changes are even more suspect, since they seem to have been demanded as a condition of publication by an Appleton editor fearful of offending public taste. The major changes in the 1895 publication, apart from a series of verbal revisions, include the dropping altogether of the original Chapter 12, the deletion of endings to Chapters 7, 10, and 15, and the heavy cutting of Chapters 16 and 25.

Until the past decade, readers have generally relied on the text published by Appleton, and most critics have otherwise accepted it as Crane's "final intention." Yet this review should suggest how serious are the questions that remain about that text, and those wishing to pursue them further should consult the essays by Binder, Bowers, Howarth, Levenson, and Pizer listed in the Selected Bibliography. In 1982, Henry Binder prepared a critical text that, despite the absence of manuscript pages, effectively reconstructed the "novel that Crane wrote." The five authors of the essays collected here have relied on Binder's reconstruction, which includes the original Chapter 12 excised in Appleton's 1895 publication. For ease of reference, and when confusion may arise, chapter citations in this collection will also include a slash reference – first to the Binder text now published by Avon, and then to the Appleton text upon which all other publishers currently rely (e.g., Chap. 16/15).

1

Introduction

LEE CLARK MITCHELL

STEPHEN Crane burst into fame with *The Red Badge of Courage* (1895) at the age of only twenty-three. Readers on both sides of the Atlantic applauded, marveling that an author too young to have known war had written about it so compellingly. And as if to confirm for himself the authenticity of his novel, Crane rushed off to battle at the first opportunity, arousing public interest in a life that came to seem even more exciting than his fiction. Like other American writers from Poe through Hemingway, he became something of an invented cultural figure – an exotic adventuring in war and in love, plagued periodically by the effects of drugs and of syphilis. Unlike their stories, however, few of his resembled his experience, and what interests us now in Crane is precisely his active fostering of biographical confusion. He seems to have enjoyed contradiction in his life even more fully than in his art, repudiating assorted conventional labels out of an irrepressible impulse toward self-revision. As Ford Madox Ford wryly observed: "I have known him change his apparent personality half a dozen times in the course of an afternoon."[1] Crane still remains elusive, both as biographical figure and as literary artist, and for reasons remarkably similar, requiring similar kinds of caution. The contradictions and repudiations that characterized his behavior, even the abbreviated nature of his career, are qualities repeated in his prose and poetry, with the collective effect of casting dubiety upon nearly all claims about him or his art.

Perhaps the best way to organize uncertainty is by separating problematic issues into three major questions, respectively biographical, historical, and textual: Who was Stephen Crane? Why did *The Red Badge of Courage* win such immediate acclaim? What in

1

fact *is* the novel? Unusual as these questions appear when directed to a major author, in this case they soon seem curiously apt. To begin with, little about the man stands unchallenged amid his friends' conflicting accounts and his own contradictory poses. And given the intimate connection that Crane himself perceived between the ordering principles of life and of art, we can best start to understand his novel by establishing certain terms about its author. In turn, the novel's extraordinary reception makes it an historical as well as a literary event, prompting a consideration of its status not only as an American classic but as a popular best-seller. How could Crane's contemporaries have reveled in a novel that, from our perspective, so subverts their assumptions?

This paradox may in its own turn result from the problem of identifying a reliable text. After all, two radically different versions of *Red Badge* appeared within a year of each other, neither of which may have been the one that Crane actually intended. With a novel so ambiguous that one is hard put to discern when the narrative voice wavers between pathos and irony, the question of whether the text is reliable assumes far greater importance than it might otherwise. That few until recently have made sure of their text before venturing a spectrum of critical views only seems of a piece with the assorted biographical errors that many have continued to accept. Ironically, Crane's fiction itself repeatedly illustrates the hazards of interpretation, and it is fitting that with no one else so fully does the author's life, his novel's reception, even the novel itself, finally resist evaluation.

1

His biographers should be forgiven their mistakes in the light of Crane's misrepresentations; their frequent addition of a year to his age, for instance, merely repeats his own error on his last birthday. Over and over, those reconstructing his life have been baffled by his contradictory self-descriptions, and too often were lured into making conclusions that were overturned by later evidence or less problematic interpretations. We can nonetheless confidently assert that of all American writers now considered great, Crane was the shortest-lived and produced the smallest body of important work.

Between the printing of *Maggie* in 1893 and his death in 1900 from tuberculosis, he wrote one major novel, a handful of important stories, and two small, though remarkable, books of poetry. The very brevity of a career we think of as major directs our attention to his literary and social context and to the important fact that Crane came of age as Victorian social values were themselves coming under attack. Few were more vigorous than writers in protesting the straitjacket of genteel standards of decorum, and in the 1880s dozens of young authors began to repudiate social taboos and specious verbal usage. One need not agree with H. L. Mencken in dating all modern American literature from Crane to allow that his work does neatly define the twin directions fiction would take because of that rebellion – toward social realism, on the one hand, and symbolic impressionism, on the other.

Stephen Crane began life on November 1, 1871, as the fourteenth child of devout Newark, New Jersey, Methodists. His father, the Reverend Jonathan Crane, died when Stephen was only eight – a fact that has not prevented some from concluding Crane's rebellious personality resulted from his resistance to paternal constraints. A "preacher's kid," so the story goes, Crane rebelled against religious pieties and middle-class standards by flagrantly taking up smoking and drinking. Yet a different reason for this rebellious image emerges in the excuse he offered for adolescent beer drinking: "How was I going to know what it tasted like less'n I tasted it? How you going to know about things at all less'n you *do* 'em?"[2] Perhaps this taste for experiment suggests why Crane was a notoriously poor student, who in failing semesters at Lafayette College and Syracuse University distinguished himself at poker, billiards, and baseball far more than he did at his studies. And it may also help explain why he pursued an interest begun during his summers as a teen-age reporter for his brother's Asbury Park press bureau. No simple explanation emerges, however, for Crane's decision to break with accepted news style. Throughout his journalistic career, his impressionistic prose invariably sent tremors through the city room, where editors recognized how easily his pieces could scandalize as well as energize their middle-class readers.

The independence of Crane's journalistic style was matched by a fascination with unusual fictional subjects, leading him as an undergraduate to write about life in New York City's Bowery district. Even in this first draft of *Maggie*, moreover, Crane broke with the usual narrative conventions, later prompting some to observe that he wrote as if the literary tradition from Shakespeare to James simply did not exist. That Tolstoy, Kipling, and Poe, among others, did indeed have an influence upon him hardly alters the accuracy of William Dean Howells's friendly toast to a writer who had "sprung into life fully armed." Nor was Crane averse to reinforcing that impression. Following a characteristic American pattern, he sought to dissociate himself from the apparently ineffectual role of author and intellectual. When asked about Mallarmé, for instance, he allegedly answered, "I don't know much about Irish authors" – a response as arch as it may have been honest. The determination to appear other than self-consciously literary nonetheless flew in the face of Crane's clear devotion to his craft.

Failing to persuade a publisher of its merit, Crane finally printed *Maggie* at his own expense under the pseudonym of Johnston Smith. The publishers had in fact been right in predicting that no notice would be taken of this first work of American naturalism, and its author found that he could hardly give away the novel of a slum girl's fall to prostitution, then suicide. Crane himself now fell into genteel poverty, eased by borrowing, cadging, and free-lance journalism, and he suffered through the economic panic of 1893 with a group of other New York City bohemians. To escape destitution, he conceived the idea of a best-selling war novel, and turned for material to the first-person accounts in *Century Magazine*'s once-popular series on "Battles and Leaders of the Civil War." Yet after reading a while, the lifeless chronicling of facts, numbers, and names surprised him: "I wonder that *some* of these fellows don't tell how they *felt* in those scraps!" he exclaimed. "They spout eternally of what they *did*, but they are as emotionless as rocks!"[3] Perhaps he recalled a military school teacher who had been famous for bringing Civil War battles alive for students. Or he may have been prompted by Zola's supposedly inadequate account of war in *La Débâcle*. But whatever the inspiration – whether poverty, subject matter, literary rivalry, or a combination of causes – he soon discovered that the material resisted a formulaic treatment: "I deliberately started in to do a potboiler, something that would take the boarding-school element – you know the kind. Well, I got interested in the thing in spite of myself, and I couldn't, I couldn't! I *had* to do it my own way."[4] That "way," moreover, involved a radical transition from *Maggie* in the shift from a third-person perspective to the free indirect discourse that reveals impressions all but firsthand. Crane dramatizes "the youth's" experiences directly instead of neutrally describing events, anticipating Ford Madox Ford's dictum to "render, never report."

Crane began writing no later than March 1893, and that summer completed his most sustained effort even as he was scraping by with occasional journalism and composing the remarkable poems that became the *Black Riders* (1895). Rebuffed once again by publishers, he turned this time to the Bacheller-Johnson news syndicate, which accepted the 55,000-word manuscript on the condition that it be severely abridged. In December 1894, a version one-third of the original first appeared in hundreds of newspapers nationwide, and despite Crane's mixed feelings about its radical amputation, the novel created the enthusiastic stir he had been hoping for all along. As well, it had the effect of interesting the publishing house of D. Appleton and Company, which brought out a longer version of the novel the following October.

In both Britain and America, *The Red Badge of Courage* was greeted by what H. G. Wells termed an "orgy of praise." It went through ten editions in its first year alone, through as many more in the next dozen, and was accorded a critical reception unusual for the work of a living writer. Mere days after its publication, an anonymous reviewer struck a note that would be sounded by countless others: "At times the description is so vivid as to be almost suffocating. The reader is right down in the midst of it where patriotism is dissolved into its elements and where only a dozen men can be seen, firing blindly and grotesquely into the smoke. This is war from a new point of view."[5] However uncertain readers may have felt in identifying the narrative causes of such powerful effects, most felt assured in their admiration: "Not the least of Mr. Crane's gifts is that this narrative, with scarce a name to hang upon a single character, and no plot whatsoever, holds one irreversibly. There is no possibility of resistance, when once you are in its grip" (93). This reviewer, moreover, concluded that the author's "insight and his power of realization amount to genius." Indeed, the most striking aspect of these initial raves is the frequency with which words like "genius" and "masterpiece" occur – perhaps to help account for the surprise that someone so innocent of battle had captured its inimitable smell.

Of course, a few turned Crane's alleged inexperience against him, condemning the novel that "bristles more with false grammar than with bayonets" (159). And often as not, they seized upon strained rationales to defend their genteel critiques: "He did not spend much time at school, which probably accounts for his grammatical lapses and for many faults of style" (123). Others merely assumed that Crane's youthfulness had led to historical inaccuracies. Most notoriously, a Civil War veteran, General Alexander C. McClurg, fulminated against the novel as "a vicious satire upon American soldiers and American armies" (140). That most others disagreed with such verdicts is less remarkable than that the occasional words of condemnation can themselves so often be seen as inadvertent praise. One critic, upset at the novel's staccato prose, claimed that "the short, sharp sentences hurled without sequence give one the feeling of being pelted from different angles by hail – hail that is hot" (97). Crane himself would have welcomed this otherwise dismissive characterization.

It took one singular reader, however, to assess the narrative reasons for the effect of Crane's prose, and George Wyndham's review within three months of the novel's appearance set an interpretive standard that lasted for over a quarter of a century. Wyndham started by recognizing that Crane was "a great artist, with something new to say, and consequently, with a new way of saying it" (108) – echoing the phrase Crane himself had used in recalling his effort ("my own way"). Crane had adopted a narrative "compromise," Wyndham noted, to highlight the vivid impressions of a youth in battle. His review astutely explores the observation that Crane "stages the drama of war, so to speak, within the mind of one man, and then admits you as to a theatre." Wyndham was praised by, among others, the novelists Joseph Conrad and Harold Frederick for having helped them define their own stunned admiration of a novel that defied customary categories. As Frederick, in his own review, pointed out: "If there were in existence any books of a similar character, one could start confidently by saying that it was the best of its kind. But it has no fellows. It is a book outside of all classification. So unlike anything else is it that the temptation rises to deny that it is a book at all" (116).

Much as *Red Badge* seemed unlike a traditional book, Crane experienced what was still an untraditional pattern of overnight success. Interest immediately sprang up in both his recently published poems and his earlier fiction, and now his well-known by-line ensured that no matter how often expenses exceeded income, he would never be destitute. More importantly, fame transformed his life itself by presenting opportunities that made his last four years rather bizarre. Sent to Mexico in January 1895 with the injunction to report anything he wanted, Crane spent five months on the road. He met the undergraduate Willa Cather in Lincoln, Nebraska; witnessed a blizzard and barroom brawl that formed the basis for "The Blue Hotel"; and made a hair-raising escape from Mexican bandits later fictionalized in "One Dash – Horses." Hired the following year by William Randolph Hearst to report on a Cuban insurrection, Crane joined other filibusterers shipping out of Jacksonville, Florida, on New Year's Eve 1896. The *Commodore* sank on their second night out, and Crane bravely helped others escape before leaping with the captain and two others into a dinghy. Their full day and night on the winter Atlantic formed the most hazardous episode of his life, inspiring as well what most readers have agreed is his finest story, "The Open Boat."

Three months later, Crane rushed off to Greece to report on the war with Turkey; then in 1898 he covered the Spanish-American War, having finally succeeded in reaching Cuba for Joseph Pulitzer and Puerto Rico for Hearst. That he wrote some of the best wartime dispatches even his fellow journalists conceded; yet neither could they ignore the reportorial behavior that seemed nothing less than a courtship of death. More than merely risking his troubled health in debilitating semitropical conditions, he exposed himself to combat fire daringly, repeatedly, and altogether unnecessarily. Crane's relations with women were likewise unconventional and likewise self-destructive, culminating in 1896 with his gentlemanly defense of an alleged streetwalker. His quixotic gallantry irritated the police into hounding him from New York City and evoked condemnation even from those who admired both him and his writing – including the youthful police commissioner himself, Teddy Roosevelt. His reputation was marred more seriously a year later when he attached himself to Cora Howarth, the madam of a Jacksonville pleasure palace called the Hotel de Dream. Cora's estranged husband refused a divorce, and the unmarried couple felt compelled to escape from provincial constraints by moving to England. The dilapidated manor they rented at Brede Place could hardly have been worse for Crane's health, and even a literary climate enlivened by neighbors like Conrad, Ford, James, and Wells could not assuage the ill effects of the damp Surrey air. For nearly a year, he suffered from the later stages of malarial infestation and tuberculosis before dying on June 5, 1900. Howells had written Crane four years earlier that he was glad "you are getting your glory young."[6] Little could he have known that the writer who would not reach twenty-nine would get it no other way.

In general, then, what can be said of a life so intensely at odds with itself? A man who scorned vainglory in his fiction and who otherwise scoffed at chivalrous action, Crane nonetheless acted in numerous episodes in what can only be termed a heroic manner. Gallantry distinguished his behavior in the sinking of the *Commodore*, just as his fearlessness in battle impressed even Richard Harding Davis, the first man to popularize the role of dashing war correspondent. Repeatedly risking his life under fire, strolling in a white raincoat on a crest above the battlefield, Crane became something of a war hero himself. Yet one might well ask why the very issues treated with deft irony in his prose – of bravery and the challenge of death – emerged so straightforwardly in his behavior. Was it that his fiction could dismiss such efforts because experience had taught him their terms so well? Had his very defiance of fear, that is, given him a fuller understanding of the limits of the self?

All we can legitimately conclude is that Crane's was simply a contradictory nature, so contradictory as to shape even his ethical considerations. From his school days, he had been fiercely devoted to the notion of fair play, and a classmate would fondly recall that he possessed "poor genius, the insane idea that the world might be regulated by justice."[7] His fictional denunciations of universal values, and particularly of some form of ultimate justice, conflicted with his clear attraction to the possibility. Similarly, his celebrated courtliness seems curious in someone so opposed to his society's mores. "In spite of his devotion to realism in literature," another friend wrote, he "was incurably romantic about women, and this extended even to the girl of the streets."[8] He sneered at proscriptions against "fallen" women, and yet he confirmed social custom by placing them on pedestals. In the same contradictory light, his self-portrayal as hard-bitten man of the world conflicts with accounts of his kindly humor and wry self-deprecation. He was, more than most, a man of paradoxical poses that led to a reputation he did not deserve. And although he actively sought to discern the rules by which behavior might be ordered, he later became aware of how extreme were the consequences of his disorderly impulse: "Candidly, I was worse than I should have been but I always had a singular faculty of having it said that I was engaged in crimes which are not of my accomplishments."[9]

Crane was finally victimized by fame, which freed him to perfect his art only by imprisoning him in a style of life that took its toll on his writing. Recognition then vanished as quickly as it had appeared, leaving him all but forgotten for two decades after his death. Perhaps understandably, World War I had the effect of renewing interest in *Red Badge*, and the Modern Library's publication in 1921 of a popular collection of his fiction prepared the way two years later for Thomas Beer's biography. Neither that major study, however, nor the twelve-volume edition of collected works that Alfred Knopf published later in the decade is any longer considered reliable. Beer self-consciously fiddled with the evidence in order to rehabilitate Crane's sullied reputation, and Knopf's edition is equally unrigorous in matters of textual accuracy. More importantly if mysteriously, this revival of popular interest in Crane failed to engage the scholarly community. Not until 1950 was critical attention aroused by the nearly simultaneous publication of William M. Gibson's collection of essays and John Berryman's biography. Berryman, moreover, provocatively linked the art with the life, and despite a reductive Freudianism, his bifocal perspective has shaped most subsequent studies of Crane's career.

It should be clear that the quarrels among Crane's biographers result less from them than from their elusive subject, whose willing experiments and self-revisions were prompted by a temperament at once moral and fatalistic. "I understand that a man is born into the world with his own pair of eyes," Crane asserted in a frequently quoted claim, "and he is not at all responsible for his vision – he is merely responsible for his quality of personal honesty. . . . This aim in life struck me as being the only thing worth while. A man is sure to fail at it, but there is something in the failure."[10] This conjunction of "vision" and "responsibility," of "honesty" and "failure," importantly defines the terms of a life that challenged everyday assumptions and helps us to understand a body of fiction that likewise subverts received literary conventions. Joseph Conrad first recognized in Crane a temperament that "makes all things new and new things amazing," and it is this radical freshness that readers find at once so engaging and yet so disorienting.[11] Predictably, Crane offered no theory by which to comprehend his unsettling fictions, nor did he articulate any system to his preferences and antipathies. He may have allied himself sympathetically with Howells and Hamlin Garland, sharing with them a willingness "to express myself in the simplest and most concise way."[12] But his fiction itself is altogether unlike theirs in either technique or subject matter, and we now need some other way to explore the terms of Crane's art.

2

The most astonishing turn in Crane's brief career was the enthusiastic reception accorded *The Red Badge of Courage*. After all, a once enormous interest in the Civil War had receded in three decades after Appomatox, and one could not have anticipated its renewed attractiveness as subject matter for another novel. As a novel, moreover, Crane's work violated nearly all the criteria for best-selling success. Romances were popular as never before, and relied upon plots with a moral purpose written in language that took a lofty tone. Writers like Thomas Bailey Aldrich, Francis Marion

Crawford, and Anthony Hope turned staple formulas into best-selling commodities and established a context of expectations for fiction that helps explain the virtual stillbirth of *Maggie*.

How then to explain the novel's success except in partially circular terms, of readers' desire for more substantial fare than the general run of romantic escapism? That desire was stirred, if indirectly, by a series of nationwide transformations – transformations dramatically punctuated by the economic depressions that began in 1873 and 1893 (successively the worst the nation had known). The middle class cherished a set of powerfully rising material expectations, encouraged by a new consumer ethos and the rapid transition to finance capitalism. Yet as the poor multiplied geometrically and a diminished elite grew geometrically richer, conditions for many altered radically for the worse. As never before or since, immigration produced intolerable overcrowding in urban slums. Religious, racial, and class tensions were exacerbated by an apparently ruthless industrialization of labor, which resulted in riots and strikebreakings known today by the names of Haymarket, Homestead, and Pullman. And even those who remained behind on the newly mechanized farms saw a record number of foreclosures. Amid so many symptoms of national disease, the gaiety of the Gay Nineties might well have seemed rather thin. A grass-roots populism matured and faded, whereas the socially liberal Progressive movement gained early strength – both of them responses to laissez-faire policies of a government committed to big business, not laboring poor. The old civic virtues of stewardship and yeoman independence seemed irrelevant to the new Social Darwinists, who preached a logic of "survival of the fittest" that the middle class found self-justifyingly attractive.

This context provides a certain significance to the fact that among the most vocal admirers of *Red Badge* were the newspapermen who had read it first. Standards of journalism were in the process of being severely altered by Pulitzer and Hearst, who concerned themselves less with a genteel tradition than with "scooping" a story – less with extolling republican ideals than with energetic muckraking exposés. Their legions of paid correspondents were, many of them, disposed to cynical interpretations, having grown aware of the disparity between the harsh daily

11

grind of the "other half" and the bland pulpit pieties and patriotic slogans. That Crane's novel avoided such rhetoric aligned it with their own unadorned prose, allowing them more fully to savor the qualities they admired in his free-lance accounts. If journalists and editors "were impressed by the pungencies that annoyed them," as John Berryman observed, that respect was fully manifested in the response accorded his Civil War novel.[13]

Journalism was not only changing from what it had been just a decade before, but was assuming an institutional form just as literature was similarly consolidating. Howells, James, and Twain, like others, conceived of their efforts in newly professional terms – as contributing to a writing career that demanded mastery of certain standards of craft. The new realists claimed to take literature as a social institution more seriously than had their romantic precursors by rejecting the formulaic themes that had characterized popular fiction for most of the nineteenth century. Despite the popular preference for sentimental escapism, then, the realists committed themselves to making critiques of everyday American life. In 1885, for instance, *Century Magazine* serialized *Adventures of Huckleberry Finn, The Rise of Silas Lapham,* and *The Bostonians* simultaneously with the "Battles and Leaders" accounts that Crane would find so inadequate. Each of these novels transgressed formula with varying degrees of popular success in the effort to expose an American idealism that seemed a veneer over social discontent. And although Crane's differences with these writers were substantial, he contributed no less than they to the process by which literature was defining itself against a popular tradition.

Given this broad array of conflicts between institutions, classes, and modes of expression, it may well have been that *The Red Badge of Courage* sparked enthusiasm by defying expectations without seeming to do so. The absence of romantic conventions that had led General McClurg to condemn Crane's ignorance of war prompted others to assume that he had served at their sides – or, in the confident words of another veteran: "I was with Crane at Antietam."[14] His triumph lay in avoiding direct statement. By simply giving a callow protagonist impressions at odds with his reasoned assumptions, Crane tacitly exposed the youth's flimsy idealism. Traditional narrative structures do not insulate the reader from the violence Fleming experiences, nor do moral tags other-wise cushion the blows, as they do in conventional narratives. Most importantly, this unusual strategy is subversive only by im-plication, suggesting that the novel's very absence of authorial judgment – its seeming ability to have things both ways – led directly to its popular success. On the one hand, the lack of textual signposts made the novel seem unusually immediate; on the other, readers who succumbed to a contemporary sentimentality could reinscribe pieties into the text. The hero's hopeful conclu-sions, in short, could be read as the novel's own.

As we have seen, only a handful first realized how radically Crane was defying fictional conventions or how fully he had aban-doned the basic units that traditionally made a story a story. Plot disappears in the same way that social organization seems to be forgotten, and character in the novel is made to appear less a fixed psychological entity than a construct the reader creates. By aban-doning familiar novelistic ploys, Crane achieved a more vivid dra-matization of impressions. And by highlighting the power of lan-guage as language, he exposed the sheer vacuity of popular storytelling assumptions. Crane's fiction unsettles the customary associations between external conditions and emotional response, and in the process tests the ability of consciousness to accommo-date experience. Moreover, as if to intensify the vivid effect of the battlefield itself, *Red Badge* refuses to shift the narrative focus away from its central situation. Crane's was in fact the first novel com-pletely devoted to the experience of war, the first that failed to divert attention through domestic subplots and comic relief. Mar-tial accounts, to be sure, extend all the way back to the *Iliad,* and even the Civil War had been realistically depicted by authors like J. W. De Forest, Joseph Kirkland, and Ambrose Bierce. But no one before had presented its effects in so intensely sustained a fashion.

In a period troubled by the seemingly irresistible forces of a new international industrialism, Crane created characters now com-pelled by conditions largely outside their control – whether war, as in this novel, or the shipwreck, blizzard, and slums of his other narratives. He was the first American novelist to deprive characters of moral autonomy, giving them no more than the illusion of freedom in an emotionally precarious, often violent world. And having gained a psychological immediacy by tightening his narrative focus on war itself, Crane inverted the traditional plot movement of moral education through battlefield adversity. Earlier, in *Maggie,* he had similarly parodied conventions with his inversion of rags-to-riches success, and later he would deflate such genres as the heroic sea story and the "shoot-'em-up" Western (in "The Open Boat" and "The Bride Comes to Yellow Sky"). Likewise, <u>Red Badge</u> offered not the traditional portrait of military courage but a self-deluded youth who seemed little different after battle from what he was before.

Of course, most initial readers (and many since) could not help but see Henry in conventional terms, reading the novel according to the generic expectations of a romantic war hero. That process was further ensured by the fact that the published novel seems not to have been what Crane intended. The version that had sparked attention had been cut by Bacheller to a third as long as the original, altering Henry Fleming into something other than a clearly self-centered youth. Even the fuller version that Appleton published made cuts that mask the manuscript's ironic tone and lend a more heroic color to Henry's behavior. The two first available versions, in other words, were more palatable than the full manuscript would have been to an audience still caught by old formulas. A heroizing reading of Henry Fleming may not only have contributed to the novel's popularity but may as equally have prompted life to imitate art in a return to militant imperialism. Teddy Roosevelt, for instance, believed that military action could regenerate America's flaccid moral fiber, and combined an admiration for the book with swashbuckling heroics in Cuba three years later, followed in turn by big-stick ventures into the Philippines and Panama. Resistance to the impersonal patterns fostered by a newly encroaching bureaucracy began to manifest itself in the attraction to violent experience – evidenced as much in the reception of Crane's novel as in that of the Hearst papers' reports of San Juan Hill.

None of these explanations for the novel's success breaks with a certain circular pattern, but perhaps that should not bother us. For no evidence can tell whether it was Crane's youth that contributed to the book's success or its success that drew attention to his youth

– whether *Red Badge* unsettled expectations or instead somehow confirmed them. Given the contradictions in both the author and the novel, no ready pattern emerges of cause and effect. One is left simply to recognize that Crane's masterpiece created its popular audience even as that audience created it.

3

Although an author's life might seem elusive and the reasons for his success obscure, his published text itself usually appears to be straightforward. Yet nothing could be less true of *The Red Badge of Courage,* the very history of whose readings is, arguably, one of distortion, invention, and mistaken assumptions. Indeed, the novel almost disappears in a cycle of generic expectation and self-fulfilling conclusion. Part of the reason, as we have seen, is that two major versions of the novel exist (as well as the radically excerpted Bacheller text), and readers have turned to the Appleton text at least in part because the original manuscript has not been readily available. Lately, however, a few critics have questioned the numerous revisions Crane made for Appleton, persuaded by Hershel Parker's claim that the changes were compelled by an editor afraid of violating genteel standards. In the most detailed elaboration of this position, Henry Binder has argued that his painful failure with *Maggie* two years earlier, and the full year's wait with this manuscript, prompted Crane to agree to changes that controverted his final intentions.[15] Simply to get his novel published, Binder claims, Crane made a series of radical cuts involving not only potentially offensive realistic details but substantial passages of Henry Fleming's self-justifications and vapid philosophizing.

Final intentions can never be proved, and yet Binder's argument rests on more than indirect evidence and textual interpretation. Further supporting this view are what we know of Crane's personal habits, including his notorious indifference to reading proof. He wrote both his poetry and prose straight out in bursts of creative energy, amazing friends by completing whole chapters without pause or hesitation. He rarely altered a phrase or word and was fiercely impatient with the need for revision. Although he never commented on problems with his editor or attempted to publish his original text, it seems likely that Appleton did not produce Crane's intended design.

Before turning to the larger questions raised by this elusive novel, we need to define the context in which any discussion must take place. Least obviously and most certainly, the battle fought by Henry Fleming's New York regiment occurred on May 1 and 2, 1863, at Chancellorsville, Virginia. Both this particular battle and the fact that it remains unnamed throughout shape the terms of a novel that offers impressions from the point of view of a combatant. After all, few soldiers during combat think of the names of places by which history labels their efforts, or in this case realized that a later generation would define the whole as the "Civil War" (indeed, the South continues to refer to the conflict as "The War Between the States"). Naming neither battle nor war, therefore, lends a more realistic effect to the novel precisely in the absence of local specification of what otherwise is so carefully described.

Crane's selection of Chancellorsville may have owed something to the influence of his brother, who was a Civil War buff and an expert on that particular battle. Stephen could not have helped consulting Edmund during the summer he spent writing at his brother's home. But the more compelling thematic reason is that the battle so perfectly represented the dark ironies of war. Twenty-seven thousand men died in a conflict whose immediate consequences seemed nil at best and at worst senseless; the North lost despite a decided superiority, the South won a merely Pyrrhic victory, and after two days both sides were left almost exactly where they had been. From military history, Crane could hardly have chosen a more futile episode, and his novel is scrupulously accurate in detailing the movements of troops and their engagements, the weather and general geography, even the specific local terrain of hills, rivers, and marshes.

The absence of labels and dates makes the narrative more, not less, effective by shifting attention away from either historical patterns or local meanings. Instead, the novel concentrates on the emotional violence of actual battle – any battle on any ground, between two armies in any war. Compounding this narrative effect throughout is the characters' lack of names; such epithets as "the loud soldier" and "the tattered soldier" serve to dramatize the irrelevance of social categories and the arbitrariness of linguistic convention. Crane's unwillingness to attach customary labels to individuals, places, or events illuminates by contrast how much can be lost when traditional identifications *are* made, when labels *are* used to order and yet to constrain experience.

Similarly, the novel breaks down grammatical order in the illogical transitions between image and subject, the fragmented syntax that contributes to Crane's characteristically abrupt or "nervous" style. The concentration on simple sentences at the expense of complex and compound constructions evokes a world lacking interdependency, one that refuses to hang together in predictable patterns. The heavily adverbial, prepositional prose rarely defines causal connections, instead compelling from the reader interpretations to fit the welter of images. Indeed, Crane reestablishes through stylistic means the primacy of sensory experience and implicates the reader in undifferentiated emotions through repetition and a stripping of diction. The very opening paragraph brings the narrative world alive, as the awakening army is imbued with an animistic sense. And thereafter, language refuses to insulate the reader by domesticating into familiar patterns the urgency of experience it represents.

Once alerted to the importance of its setting and having noted the implications of its wrenching style, we cannot fail to see the significance of the novel's strikingly dual structure. Nearly everything is repeated with formal precision, as two days of battle appear in twenty-five chapters that divide near the middle at Chapter 13/12, when Henry Fleming receives the "red badge" of an accidental head wound. The first twelve chapters expose his seeming cowardice, and his apparent heroism emerges in the last dozen. In turn, both halves of the novel divide, as the enemy charges twice in the opening half and on the second occasion panics Henry into flight; the motion is reversed in the last twelve chapters, when his own regiment charges twice and finally frightens the enemy into flight. Not to belabor a description of multiple other doublings and repetitions, the question they raise remains unchanged and central to the novel's interpretation. Such narrative mirroring can potentially show possibilities for an individual's growth and maturity, clarifying the development of certain traits by keeping the contexts the same. Alternatively, from an ironic perspective, such doubling can as easily expose the absence of genuine growth and dramatize how fully all stays unchanged despite superficially quite different results.

Either interpretation, in any event, must confront what John Berryman called Crane's "refusal to guarantee."[16] Whether at the specific level of diction or in larger terms of narrative endings, he leaves things inconclusive. As well, by subtly disrupting literary conventions, he presents an analogue for his readers of the very experience his characters face. Just as Henry Fleming cannot help interpreting his own ambiguous impulses, so the reader arrives at a novelistic "meaning" in the automatic process of deciphering Crane's grammar. That the reader's conclusions, like Henry's, depend on essentially conventional expectations reveals no more than that all interpretations are imposed upon chaotic experience and unruly texts. This has not, of course, always been clear to those offering to interpret the novel, which makes the history of its readings instructive for those coming to it afresh. Among his early admirers, for instance, both Edward Garnett and Joseph Conrad first recognized Crane as a literary "impressionist" – or as Conrad asserted: "*the only* impressionist and *only* an impressionist."[17] Neither one pursued this painterly analogy, and not until half a century later would the formalist New Critics probe its implications by examining the use in *Red Badge* of color imagery and synesthetic conceits. By revealing the novel's poetic complexities through a variety of close textual analyses, they exposed, sometimes inadvertently, its severe ambiguities.

A few critics have explored the novel in terms of Christian allegory, basing their readings on the suggestive initials and dramatic death of Jim Conklin and, in particular, on the concluding sentence of Chapter 9: "The sun was pasted in the sky like a fierce wafer." Accepting war as a process that contributes to man's final redemption, these interpreters have followed Robert W. Stallman's lead in reading the novel as a modern wasteland through which Henry Fleming wanders as a kind of Everyman. Freudians, on the other hand, have cleared the trail John Berryman first blazed by viewing the novel in largely Oedipal terms. Henry's outrage at a

18

pattern of senseless violence is construed as a narrative enactment of Crane's own belated resistance to his parents' Methodist pieties and of the sense of betrayal he supposedly felt at his father's early death. Still others have read Crane in a literary-historical context that emphasizes his stature as a naturalist, comparing *Red Badge* with his other works as well as with the fiction of contemporaries like Theodore Dreiser, Frank Norris, and Jack London. In a universe where ineluctable forces control the individual, Henry Fleming becomes merely the victim of impulse and event, unable to enact a will that might break through fundamentally determinist patterns. Structuralists have more recently examined the verbal patterns of the novel to reveal the degree to which Henry arbitrarily projects a conventional moral-linguistic code onto the chaos of experience. His failure becomes one of interpretation, not action, and consists of his inability to recognize the reality he suffers as a verbal contrivance he himself has helped to make.

Nearly all readings converge on the question of Crane's irony and specifically on the process by which the novel's central character is shaped and presented. Simply put, is Henry Fleming a hero or not? And if not, does he nonetheless mature through the novel? These interrelated questions emerge most fully in the novel's final chapter, where Henry reviews his behavior during that day's battle and recalls his "cowardly" flight the day before. His growth may have seemed assured for readers of the Appleton text, especially since its final chapter severely edits his inflated rationalizings. Still, the fact that these self-reflections strongly resemble his mood in Chapter 16/15 suggests that he has gained little maturity. In some ways, the later scene makes him seem even more subtly self-deluded, since his attitude toward himself, toward Wilson, and toward nature controverts the novel's dramatized claims. A narrative that itself is never less than contingent everywhere subverts Henry's own smug sense that he has achieved the conventional status of a hero. Just as he never accommodates himself to the recognition of nature's indifference, the novel's last lines suggest his inability to acquire adequate self-recognition. By posing his existence as "not inconsequent to the sun," he suggests a self-assurance little different from his occasional posture in the novel's first half. Yet no contradicting narrator at this point steps forward, nor does a neutral omniscient tone appear, and the irony of his bombast can be lost in the pathos of his point of view.

Recurrent as is Henry's self-satisfaction, it forms only one strain of the novel, and no more here than elsewhere does Crane authorize a single perspective. Wilson's transition, for instance, from being a "loud soldier" to generous self-deprecation – or the more vivid instance of the unseen "cheery soldier" who guides Henry back to his regiment – offer dramatic alternatives to his own egotistical reflections. The sole (if hardly saving) grace in this kind of indifferent, violent world lies in the capacity for just such gestures of self-transcendent loyalty and kindness.

The Red Badge of Courage tests us nearly as much as it does Henry Fleming, eliciting judgments that in turn judge us more than is true of most fictional texts. Yet to recognize that it successfully exposes the assumptions by which we interpret experience is not to surrender to a view of the novel's total indeterminacy. What it should encourage is rather a healthy caution in the assertions we finally do make about the novel, and in the process it should induce in us a sense of Crane's own wonder at the chaos of experience. Ever recognizing life's multiform possibilities, he went from Bowery to battlefront, Mexican standoffs to manor living, in the continuing effort to satisfy a lively curiosity. The risks he took with unnecessary hazards may well speak to a subliminal death wish, but they also suggest a need momentarily to break free from the conventions that always define us. Crane attempted to break free as well from a whole host of literary assumptions, and his work forms a perfect counterpart to his life in their joint resistance to interpretation – which makes it easier to agree on what he is not than on what he is. At the end of a long review of the recently dead young author, H. G. Wells observed: "He began stark . . . as though he came into the world of letters without ever a predecessor. In style, in method, and in all that is distinctively *not* found in his books, he is sharply defined, the expression in literary art of certain enormous repudiations."[18] In approaching his most famous novel, we must keep those "enormous repudiations" before us, and perhaps the most compelling aspect of the following essays is that each of them succeeds in doing so.

From the vantage of the textual scholar, Hershel Parker argues for

20

the manuscript Crane originally wrote as the one that best represents his intended design. He examines the history of Crane's experience with editors, his trouble publishing both *Maggie* and *Black Riders,* and the literary politics involved in getting any of his original versions accepted – whether in the 1890s or the 1980s – establishing in the process the textual problems every reader needs initially to confront in *Red Badge.* Its uniqueness as a war novel is what interests Andrew Delbanco, who focuses on its unusual narrative progressions to reveal a peculiarly American concern with reclaiming political and spiritual ideals. Crane was trying, like his minister father, to find "reasons to be pious about America," and the novel only more dramatically reveals what he expressed throughout his career: the wistful longing for a sense of community that was diminishing as a possibility even as he wrote. Amy Kaplan turns more directly to the context of the 1890s, and with similar sensitivity to the novel's disruptive prose shows its challenge to those assumptions most deeply cherished by his contemporaries. Specifically, by presenting warfare as a spectacle and yet by questioning any terms within which that spectacle might be accommodated, Crane offered a profound critique of the newly emergent forces of militant imperialism. Howard C. Horsford explores the novel's double perspective and reveals how the shifts in Henry Fleming's disposition are echoed in the various shifts of the narrative – most prominently in the alternation between a personal and a cosmic voice. Regardless of which version of the novel one reads, Horsford argues, this persistent deferral of resolution undermines any conclusion that Henry's final assurance has been earned. Christine Brooke-Rose concludes similarly on the basis of the novel's multiple verbal polarities, all of which are subsumed in the carefully wrought opposition between courage and cowardice. Through a deconstructive reading of these oppositions, she shows that the novel exposes the irony of not only Henry's self-confidence, but of any attempt at a novel about war.

The most authoritative although seriously flawed biography is R. W. Stallman's *Stephen Crane: A Biography* (New York: George Braziller, 1968). The two best overviews of his critical reception, both published on the centennial of Crane's birth, are Stanley Wertheim's bibliographical essay in *Hawthorne, Melville, Stephen*

Crane: A Critical Bibliography (New York: Free Press, 1971), pp. 203–301; and Donald Pizer's essay in *Fifteen American Authors Before 1900*, ed. Robert A. Rees and Earl N. Harbert (Madison: University of Wisconsin Press, 1971), pp. 97–137. Also useful are Pizer's subsequent essay, "Stephen Crane: A Review of Scholarship and Criticism Since 1969," *Studies in the Novel* 10 (1978):120–45; and Marston La France, "Stephen Crane Scholarship Today and Tomorrow," *American Literary Realism* 7 (Spring 1974):125–35. For provocative excerpts from contemporary reviews of *Red Badge*, see R. W. Stallman, *Stephen Crane: A Critical Bibliography* (Ames: Iowa State University Press, 1972), pp. 84–105.

The following collections of essays include important discussions of the novel: *The Red Badge of Courage*, ed. Sculley Bradley et al., 2nd ed. (New York: Norton, 1976); *Stephen Crane: A Collection of Critical Essays*, ed. Maurice Bassan (Englewood Cliffs, N.J.: Prentice-Hall, 1967); *Stephen Crane: The Critical Heritage*, ed. Richard M. Weatherford (London: Routledge & Kegan Paul, 1973); *Stephen Crane's Career: Perspectives and Evaluations*, ed. Thomas A. Gullason (New York: New York University Press, 1972); and "Special Number: Stephen Crane," *Studies in the Novel* 10 (Spring 1978).

NOTES

1. "Stevie," *The Literary Review of the New York Evening Post*, July 12, 1924, p. 882. Cited by Thomas A. Gullason, Introduction to *The Complete Novels of Stephen Crane*. (Garden City, N.Y.: Doubleday, 1967), p. 19.
2. This anecdote is recorded by R. W. Stallman in *Stephen Crane: A Biography* (New York: George Braziller, 1968), p. 12.
3. C. K. Linsom, *My Stephen Crane*, ed. Edwin H. Cady (Syracuse, N.Y.: Syracuse University Press, 1958), p. 37.
4. *Stephen Crane: Letters*, ed. R. W. Stallman and Lillian Gilkes (New York: New York University Press, 1960), p. 319.
5. Cited in Richard M. Weatherford, ed. *Stephen Crane: The Critical Heritage* (London: Routledge & Kegan Paul, 1973), p. 86. Subsequent references to reviews will be to this text and indicated parenthetically.
6. Stallman and Gilkes, ed., *Letters*, p. 102.

7. See Stallman, *Biography*, pp. 21–2.
8. Stallman and Gilkes, ed., *Letters*, p. 333.
9. Ibid., p. 209.
10. Ibid., p. 110.
11. Ibid., p. 154.
12. Ibid., p. 158. See also pp. 31, 127, and 250 for Crane's alignment of himself with Howells and Garland, yet his lack of enthusiasm for their efforts.
13. John Berryman, *Stephen Crane* (1950; rev. ed. New York: World Publishing Co., 1962), p. 34.
14. Stallman, *Biography*, p. 181.
15. Henry Binder, "The *Red Badge of Courage* Nobody Knows," in *The Red Badge of Courage* (New York: Avon, 1983), pp. 111–58.
16. Berryman, *Stephen Crane*, pp. 287–8.
17. Stallman and Gilkes, ed., pp. 154–5.
18. Ibid., p. 316.

2

Getting Used to the "Original Form" of *The Red Badge of Courage*

HERSHEL PARKER

SINCE 1975 I have been campaigning to gain readers for *The Red Badge of Courage* in the form Crane wrote it, as nearly as that can be reconstructed, rather than the form that was published in 1895. The first chores were to edit the text, study it, celebrate it, and get it into print. During the early phases of the campaign, I focused mainly on the intellectual honesty and aesthetic rewards awaiting anyone who read the book as Crane wrote it, and my then-student Henry Binder, after accounting for the 1895 truncations, also concentrated his energies on reading the book as Crane wrote it. We were, as we said, *celebrating* an unknown masterpiece. Others joined in the celebration – witness Lee Mitchell's choice of text for citations in this volume. Some have refused to celebrate, however, and it is these reluctant, skeptical souls whom I want to persuade in this essay, which is not a new celebration but an attempt – really, the first detailed attempt – to locate *The Red Badge of Courage* precisely in Crane's literary career during the years 1892–6 (if one can apply the term "career" to anything so stymied) and to focus sharply upon the precise nature of the war book that he worked on, completed, and then lived with for many months afterward. I want to back away from the controversy over the reconstructed text so that I can help us all get used to thinking of the original form of *The Red Badge of Courage*.

The story is hard to get straight. As with most important episodes in Crane's life, basic dates are hard to pin down. He apparently started his war book at about the time he turned twenty-one (November 1892), then worked on it through the next year and finished it late in 1893 or very early in 1894. The early part of this period coincided with the end of the arduous months Crane spent

25

trying to interest New York City publishers in his first novel, *Maggie: A Girl of the Streets*. During much of 1892 and probably into early 1893, Crane was rebuffed by what was hyperbolically described as "almost every" publisher in New York City. The editor Richard Watson Gilder, a man who owed Crane some kindness as an acquaintance of the young man's dead parents, was typical and explicit: He told Crane that the manuscript of *Maggie* had pained him by its "cruel" content and its extreme, uneducated style. Crane reportedly cut him off by saying, "You mean that the story's too honest?" At the house of D. Appleton, which Crane approached in due course, the manuscript was read and rejected by Ripley Hitchcock, who was later to become Crane's editor. Hitchcock was right: Appleton's reputation would have been ruined if he had published a novel in which the title character was last seen as a prostitute on the waterfront, late at night, in the company of a grotesque fat man who had followed her down from the nearest street, chuckling and leering as he went. The members of the American literary establishment were a remarkably homogeneous set of males of British ancestry and conventional upper-middle-class education, and for all the nominal allegiance they paid to literary realism, they were aesthetically timid to the point of prizing tameness over originality, and morally timid to the point of routinely censoring themselves in advance of publication. So eminent a novelist and theorist of realism as William Dean Howells valued the decorum of American letters, and the majority of the reading public depended upon the editors to keep unnecessary unpleasantness out of their homes.

Desperate to get the slum story out, Crane paid a firm to print it for him and in March 1893 received his eleven hundred or so copies of the ugly little yellow paperback. Crane said that the firm specialized in medical-religious works, so it must have had reliable compositors and proofreaders in the house, but it did him "the dirt." The company muscled him into paying an exorbitant fee, apparently on the claim that it might be liable to the charge of printing a pornographic book. It took, to be blunt, all Crane had, a little less than $1,000 – his part of his mother's estate – and the most money he was ever to have at one time. Then it did a wretched job of printing and proofreading the book. From our secure vantage point,

Crane looks more like a Port Jervis yokel than the streetwise kid we thought we knew, but we don't know the whole story; maybe other firms had refused to print the book for him at any price, and maybe printer and author alike had valid reason to fear the vice laws. It was not mere modesty that made Crane put the name Johnston Smith on the book instead of his own, and it was no accident that the printer was not identified.

Dispersing copies himself, Crane attempted to placate his hand-chosen readers before they read his novel: Habitually, almost mechanically, he inscribed the cover of presentation copies with a justification of literary realism sweetened for the shockable by a pious reference to heaven's being open to an occasional street girl. Knowing how dangerous the publishing world had considered the book, and having subsequently suffered the trials of printing it himself, Crane was not naive in wanting to smooth the way of a prospective reader. His efforts did little good. The book received, as far as we know, a single review, and the fact that it won him the respect of Hamlin Garland and William Dean Howells did not have any immediate impact on his life.

We tend now to talk as if Crane was in control of his career at this time, even though we know that in 1893 and 1894 he was living hand-to-mouth. The "hungry kid," we say, as if the hunger were all metaphorical – a not-unpleasing ache for literary achievement and a not-unconfident yearning for inevitable fame. We know to our satisfaction that Crane could at any time have lived with relatives and been fed and well clothed, and we know that when he got money, he was apt to waste it on tobacco and wine or to give it away. The reality is that during much of the time he wrote *The Red Badge of Courage*, Stephen Crane was, in winter, cold – cold as street people are. He often went about in the sleet and snow with no overcoat because he had no overcoat, and with his toes sticking out of his shoes because those were the best or only shoes he had. To be malnourished and poorly clad was bad enough, but, we need to remind ourselves, Crane was also sick. Those racking spasms of coughing his friends remembered so vividly were probably not smoker's hack or bronchitis but early symptoms of the tuberculosis that killed him.

Worse yet, Crane was under intense intellectual and aesthetic (and consequently emotional) strain. He was a very young man with brilliant experiments left on his hands. It was almost as if he were holding powerful new kinds of bombs that ought to have been patented and then detonated one by one, at a safe distance, as he finished making them. Although he printed *Maggie* in 1893, in effect it was not published, and almost no one read it during the next three years. Praise from Garland and Howells was wonderful, but it did not keep him warm for long, and it was not detailed enough to give him a sense of how the literary world might ultimately judge what he had done. Deprived of the reviews that books customarily receive, Crane was not in a position to move on with assurance. We know from studies of creativity, notably the work of the clinical psychiatrist Albert Rothenberg, that the creative process, like any other, begins, continues, and ends. In the case of creative writing, the process involves periods of intense arousal, preoccupation, anxiety, concentration, irritation, a variety of fantasy states, vainglory, self-doubt, and obsessiveness; then, if the writer lives long enough and persists hard enough, it ends. In the case of *Maggie,* a major aspect of the creative process was frustrated – the phase of cleaning up and stowing away – and the result for Crane was that *Maggie* did not quite get off his mind in the way a completed and published book normally does. The undistributed book was even tangibly around at least one of the cluttered flats that Crane used as what we would call crash pads: Lacking chairs, he and his friends sometimes sat on piles of *Maggie.* The copies were evidence of his improvidence; but, more painfully, they were heaped-up reminders to Crane that he was stuck with, stuck in, the past – a tragicomic situation for a man who was very young indeed when he began talking about not living long.

In 1893 and 1894, what reputation Crane had was simply as a young, promising journalist. Only a few people knew he had written a very strange slum novel. By mid-1894 a handful of people knew he had written an astonishing new war novel and had a sheaf of weird-looking poems, or "lines," that he wanted to publish. Almost no one knew that late in 1894 he had not only the war novel on his hands but also a new slum novel, *George's Mother.* As a reporter, he could write a story and read it in the same day's or the next day's newspaper, yet he was in the grotesquely

frustrating position of being, for all practical purposes, a closet
literary man who had recklessly overpaid to get one example of his
real writing, his literary work, into print and who now, having no
new inheritances to squander, was more than ever at the mercy of
the cautious publishing houses.

As editors, critics, and literary theorists, we tend to put ourselves
at a distance from the creative process, having been warned of the
vulgarity of longing to throb in unison with the creating writer. So
distanced, ignoring abundant evidence from publishing history,
we tend to play down the power of publishers and to assume that
a writer can hold out to have a work printed the way he wants. So
distanced, we sometimes adopt the literary theory that an author's
acceptance of a suggestion from a friend or publisher is equivalent
to a creative act – a convenient theory if we do not know or want
to know the circumstances of publication. In our sophisticated
wariness, we also tend to discount any statement a writer makes
about his intentions for a work. Often our wariness is justified, for
a writer's comments about his intentions most often come after the
completion of the work, during the marketing phase rather than
the actual composition; they are doubly dubious, subject to the
vagaries of memory and shifting imperatives. But we are not wise
when we assume, as we sometimes do, that an author's intentions
are never recoverable.

To be sure, Crane's intentions for *The Red Badge of Courage* are
not readily recoverable from what we knew before 1979 as "the
text itself." Otherwise dozens of fine critics of good will and
trained intelligence would not have written themselves into an
impasse over his intentions, arguing inconclusively that Henry
Fleming matures or does not mature in the last chapter. Yet there
is strong documentary evidence about Crane's intention during
the composition process, the period during which his intention
was being embodied in the text. Because he was so poor, Crane
wrote some of the final manuscript version on the back of sheets
he had used in a next-to-final version now known as the "draft."
What Crane did in moving a stage beyond the fifty-seven surviving
draft pages provides extraordinarily clear evidence of his intentions – weightier evidence than any "statement" he might have
made, whether an off-the-cuff comment to an interviewer or

friend or an elaborate propounding of his aesthetic views in one of those epistolary literary manifestos he used to woo older women. And the consistency of the revisions we can see by comparing the draft and the final manuscript argues very strongly for the belief that the pattern we discern here was the one that prevailed throughout the revisions.

We can be certain, on the basis of the surviving pages of the draft, that Crane's concentration was remarkably acute as he prepared the final manuscript. Many writers cannot go from one draft to another without being lured into impromptu digressions or striking out in new narrative directions. Crane was not that kind of writer. Instead, he treated the draft as a condensed notation to be filled out as he copied it. The change from draft to final version was a process of enhancement and expansion. To follow the process, we should not think so much of Crane sitting down to rewrite as of Crane sitting down to improve the work as he copied the draft. His process was to copy a few lines pretty much verbatim, seize an opportunity to make a brief but brilliant expansion, and then go on copying a few more lines. He did not revise line by line; often he did not revise even the line following a new insertion.

There is a classic essay waiting to be written on Crane as the reviser of the surviving draft pages for the final manuscript, although the project will be hampered by the loss of many pages from the draft, including all the pages after the middle of Chapter 13, and the loss of a few pages from the final manuscript. Here I merely want to emphasize the value of the surviving draft pages and the corresponding final pages as abundant proof of the consistency of Crane's intentions. In order to emphasize the nature of Crane as reviser, I adopt a formula for my longish paragraph: what Crane did in the process of expanding as he copied. As Crane copied draft page 8 onto final manuscript page 9, he gave his young enlistee a more complicated set of feelings about his mother's speech: Seeing her tear-stained face upraised in prayer, Henry feels "suddenly ashamed of his purposes." As he copied draft page 28 onto final manuscript page 34, a depiction of a march through fields and woods, Crane added a striking bit of imagery: "They were going to look at war, the red animal, war, the blood-swollen god." He also built up his portrayal of the youth by adding to his doomed demeanor an appropriate physical manifestation: "He lagged, with tragic glances at the sky." Copying from draft page 39 the description of Henry's civilian memories while waiting for battle, Crane (on final manuscript page 40) made Henry's mental state a sort of hallucinatory revery: "A thousand details of color and form surged in his mind." As he copied draft page 40 onto final manuscript page 46, Crane enhanced the psychological realism: "He stood trying to rally his faltering intellect so that he might recollect the moment when he had loaded. But he could not." Furthermore, Crane thought to add, at the foot of page 46, a reminder of this newly added concern: "He got the one glance at the foe-swarming field in front of him and instantly ceased to debate the question of his piece being loaded." As he copied page 46 onto page 53, Crane gave Henry a fine silly bit of self-congratulation: "The supreme trial had been passed. The red, formidable difficulties of war had been vanquished." On page 61 (copying from page 53) he expanded the irony, making Henry think himself not merely the enlightened man who had fled because of his superior knowledge but now the enlightened man "who looks afar in the dark" and therefore had fled because of his superior perceptions and knowledge. As he copied page 55 onto page 63, Crane expanded the behavior of the squirrel that had allowed Henry to formulate a law of nature, and he added a passage on the refusal of this "ordinary squirrel," not a philosopher-squirrel, to "stand stolidly, baring his furry belly to the missile, and die with an upward glance at the sympathetic heavens." (The addition recalls the lagging glances that Crane had already added to Henry's own repertory of adolescent attitudinizings.) As he copied page 64 onto page 73, Crane added to Henry's evasion of the tattered man the marvelous business of his picking nervously at one of his buttons and then fastening "his eyes studiously upon the button as if it were a little problem." As he copied page 85 onto page 99, Crane heightened the lurid danger the soldier expects to encounter as he confronts the universe: Instead of feeling that "it was his business to kick and scratch and bite like a child in the hands of a parent," Henry feels that "it was his business to kick and bite and give blows as a stripling in the hands of a murderer. The law was that he should fight." This handful of examples illustrates some of the effects Crane achieved in making his final copy. By following the revisions, we can be quite sure that his intentions in the final manuscript were not inchoate, were not partially confused, were not in a perilous state of flux or reflux. Crane knew what he was doing.

The final manuscript, the work that Crane finished early in 1894, was a war story that consisted of twenty-five chapters, not twenty-four, as we thought for many years; that contained fuller endings of three chapters that were truncated in the 1895 edition; and that contained a fuller and much clearer final chapter. In the endings of Chapters 7, 10, and 15, the young recruit cast himself blasphemously as challenger to or explicator of universal law. (Henry vacillated between self-pity and self-glorification, but Crane was single-minded in his depiction of the shifting moods of his young recruit.) In Chapter 12, Crane depicted the young soldier in grandiose, self-delusive combat with and presumptuous fellowship with the powers of the universe; in his most egotistical dramatizing, the soldier saw himself as "the growing prophet of a world-reconstruction." The final chapter, 25 (24 in the Appleton text), contained Crane's strongest condemnation of the youth's unfeeling egotism (even when he hears the news of a comrade's death he can only think, with glee, of his getting away with cowardice) and his ironic depiction of Fleming's delusive maturity: "He had been to touch the great death, and found that, after all, it was but the great death and was for others. He was a man."

Crane showed the war story to Garland in April, 1894, soon after the egregious Richard Watson Gilder had scolded Garland about his indecorous use of dialect; Garland, in turn, criticized *Crane's* use of dialect. Having opened himself to advice, Crane dutifully started to take it, and halfheartedly removed some of the dialect. He made a bit of a mess. (There was nothing unusual in this: Writers tend to be haphazard and impatient when they find themselves in the position of feeling duty bound to tinker with a completed manuscript at someone else's suggestion.) From the time he finished it in 1893 or early 1894, this twenty-five-chapter version was the text Crane was first eager and finally frantic to get into print.

When we talk of *The Red Badge of Courage* that Crane began

trying to get into print, therefore, we are talking about something that has almost never been seen. The only literary man who read it and later commented on it (aside from Ripley Hitchcock) was Hamlin Garland. Some details of Garland's 1914 account are probably unreliable, but his general impression is so vivid that it must be believed: When he first read the printed book, he had been struck by the fact that it lacked many "of the most notable pages of the original manuscript." Garland's privilege was great. The nearest we can approach it is through the reconstruction available since 1979, and that text lacks a few short passages and in a few other places perforce substitutes a surviving draft passage when the final form of the passage is probably lost forever. Everything Crane said about the war story after he completed it, everything he said until well into 1895, was said about the fuller version that we now can know only in this slightly imperfect form.

A few weeks into 1894, Crane thought he had the war novel placed with the new *McClure's Magazine*. For some reason (maybe he had just piled up a backlog of manuscripts fast), S. S. McClure kept it for six or eight months – no time at all for an older, secure person, but an eternity to a usually confident young man who had been assured by a couple of literary men of his genius, yet who must have doubted himself profoundly, given the fate of *Maggie*. All the while he waited for the publication of the war story, Crane was hoping for some way to resurrect *Maggie* and was also waiting for the publication of his poems. Part of the time, he was also working toward the completion of his new slum story, *George's Mother*. Months passed, months agonizing to Crane, during which the young Boston publishers who had accepted his poems, Copeland and Day, delayed publishing them. By August 1894 Crane appealed to them for news, confessing his wish to have his "out-bring all under way by early fall" – an "out-bring" that was remarkably prone not to being brought out. After stalling silently, Copeland and Day caviled about the content of the poems they had accepted. Crane wrote them on September 9, 1894: "We disagree on a multitude of points. In the first place I should absolutely refuse to have my poems printed without many of those which you just as absolutely mark 'No.' It seems to me that you cut all the ethical sense out of the book. All the anarchy, perhaps. It is the anarchy which I particularly insist upon. From the poems which you keep you could produce what might be termed a 'nice little volume of verse by Stephen Crane,' but for me there would be no satisfaction. The ones which refer to God, I believe you condemn altogether. I am obliged to have them in when my book is printed." On October 19, 1894, Copeland and Day answered Crane brusquely, itemizing seven poems they did not want to print and specifying that they would not print the volume with three of those seven in it. Crane capitulated with a terse note enclosing the title poem. He did not even negotiate for the inclusion of the four poems that Copeland and Day had not absolutely refused to publish. He wanted to keep the ethical sense and the anarchy, but he wanted, all forgivably, to be in print.

On November 15, 1894, Crane wrote Garland about his "row with the world," in which his part was to be silent and to endure: "I have just crawled out of the fifty-third ditch into which I have been cast and I now feel that I can write you a letter that wont make you ill. McClure was a Beast about the war-novel and that has been the thing that put me in one of the ditches. He kept it for six months until I was near mad. Oh, yes, he was going to use it, but – Finally I took it to Bacheller's. They use it in January in a shortened form. I have just completed a New York book that leaves Maggie at the post. It is my best thing." This New York book was *George's Mother* – which meant that by November 1894, Crane had on his hands a printed but unpublished *Maggie;* a war novel that had been unconscionably delayed and was due to appear only in newspaper excerpts; a forthcoming – shamefully expurgated – book of poems; and a new slum novel with no publisher in sight.

Of this un-brought-out "out-bring," what first got into print, in the Philadelphia *Press* of December 3–8 1894 (a month earlier than Crane had expected), was a fraction of *The Red Badge of Courage* that avoided the depictions of Henry Fleming's philosophical posturings in favor of action scenes more likely to appeal to newspaper readers. The excerpts ended with the young soldiers Fleming and Wilson happily congratulating themselves on their new reputation for bravery. When the editor of the *Press* asked to see the young author, Bacheller took the train down with Crane and witnessed the start of a literary phenomenon: "Word flew from cellar to roof that the great Stephen Crane was in the office. Editors, reporters, compositors, proofreaders crowded around him shaking his hand. It was a revelation of the commanding power of genius." Buoyed by the praise of his peers, a tough audience to incite to such appreciation, Crane called again on Ripley Hitchcock at Appleton's, somewhat more than two years after Hitchcock had rejected *Maggie*. He seems to have taken only stories with him, for in 1900 Hitchcock quoted himself as having asked, "Haven't you got something we can make a book of?" He had, as Hitchcock knew, *Maggie*, but apparently both of them were too tactful or too wary of each other to mention it. (One of the oddities of Crane scholarship is that the relationship between Crane and Hitchcock has proved so elusive. For what it's worth, I felt I understood their encounters better when I began envisioning them in an edgy dance in which, by the rules, each partner had, now and then, to approach the other closer than he wanted to.) Instead of *Maggie*, Crane spoke of the war story, which "some of the boys around the office" of the *Press* had "seemed to like." On December 18, 1894, Crane sent the newspaper clippings to Hitchcock: "This is the war story in it's [sic] syndicate form – that is to say, much smaller and to my mind much worse than its original form." Its "original form," of course, was the full manuscript version that Garland had read months before, not the truncated text Hitchcock was later to publish.

What happened to *The Red Badge of Courage* between late December 1894 and its publication by Appleton (strictly speaking, the publication of *most* of it) is difficult to establish. Maybe the best way to ease ourselves into this part of the history is to recall that something about the manuscript proved so bothersome, or even dangerous, to Hitchcock that he lied publicly about it in the *New York Times* on April 3, 1896. Indeed, Hitchcock lied with the sort of needlessly circumstantial detail that people resort to when they have one eye on what we call a hidden agenda. The occasion – to leap ahead for a moment – was the controversy over who first appreciated Crane's war novel, American or English reviewers: "D. Appleton & Co., who brought out *The Red Badge of Courage*, have watched with amusement, if not amazement, the claims of the English 'discoverers' of Mr. Crane. The true and exact history of the publication of *The Red Badge of Courage* is that it was read and accepted by D. Appleton & Co. in December, 1894, almost a year before the book was printed. It was the intention then to publish the volume immediately, but Mr. Crane was absent from the city and could not be reached conveniently when the proofs were ready, and the work was, as a consequence, delayed. The electrotype plates were all made in the Spring of 1895, but as it was deemed inadvisable to put the book on the market at that time of the year the publication was deferred until Autumn. The book was brought out on the 1st of October in this country. Although the work was copyrighted abroad at the same time, it did not appear and was not reviewed in Europe until nearly two months afterward."

The assertion that Appleton accepted the book in December 1894 is not part of any "true and exact history." Hitchcock had not accepted it even in January, when Bacheller sent Crane off to report from the Midwest and Mexico. On January 30, 1895, Crane wrote Hitchcock from St. Louis to give him his itinerary and to ask about the book, the "original form" of which the editor now had in hand: "Any news of the war story will be grateful to me. If you had not read the story, I would wish you to hear the Philadelphia Press staff speak of it. When I was there some days [weeks?] ago, I was amazed to hear the way in which they talked of it." He wanted a decision: "I will be glad to hear from you at any time." Hitchcock's offer reached Crane in Lincoln, Nebraska, on February 12(?), 1895, and Crane wrote at once: "I've just recieved [sic] your letter. I would be glad to have Appleton and Co publish the story on those terms. I am going from here to New Orleans. The Mss could be corrected by me there in short order. I shall have to reflect upon the title. I shall not be back to New York for two months." What suggestion Hitchcock had made is uncertain, but one can make a fairly safe guess. Since the main title was already *The Red Badge of Courage*, Hitchcock, reading the full manuscript, could not have escaped learning that it was ironic – not after he encountered on page 74, all blatantly, Fleming's wistful, envious yearning for a wound just big and bloody enough to impress his fellows (and not, any reader would understand, big enough to hurt much): "He wished that he, too, had a wound, a little warm red badge of courage." (Crane may already have lined out "warm.") Two or three years before, Hitchcock had found *Maggie* too threatening to publish, and now he was finding problems with the war story that he could not have anticipated from reading the newspaper clippings. The problems could be dealt with, he plainly decided, but they would have to involve some negotiations with the volatile author — negotiations best delayed until that author was in Hitchcock's office.

Crane's travels did not in fact greatly impede the progress of the arrangements. Apologizing for the inconvenience and calling himself "extremely anxious" to have Hitchcock "bring out the book," Crane on February 20 asked that Hitchcock send the manuscript to New Orleans. Hitchcock sent it by express and Crane worked on it there, as he reported from Galveston on March 8: "I sent the Ms from New Orleans. I made a great number of small corrections." Many of the "small corrections" were substitutions of epithets for proper names. Crane had vacillated over the use of this device in *Maggie* (a brilliant way of stressing the dehumanizing effects of the environment), and he continued to vacillate about whether or not to reuse it in the war novel. (This vacillation might not have occurred if *Maggie* had had a critical reception in which various reviewers might have evaluated the experiment.) In the end, Crane decided that the device was necessary in the war story if the reader was to see the soldiers as members of a blue demonstration only partially differentiated by gross characteristics of physical size or manner. In his letter Crane continued: "As to the name I am unable to see what to do with it unless the word 'Red' is cut out perhaps. That would shorten it." What bothered Hitchcock about the title, as I have said, was probably its blatant irony in the context of the entire manuscript, and Crane's laconic offer to shorten it by a three-letter word was disingenuous. Hitchcock had Crane's address in the "City of Mexico," and nothing stood in the way of his rushing the book into print under the full main title of *The Badge of Courage*. Yet he did not do so.

When Crane returned to New York City in mid-May, he found copies of the Copeland and Day *The Black Riders* waiting for him — the first time he had seen his name on a title page. Although all the "ethical sense" and "anarchy" had been purged from the book, Crane did not disown it but instead enthusiastically passed out copies to his friends and basked in his instant notoriety in which extravagantly laudatory reviews outnumbered the extravagantly hostile ones. Crane was acting the way most writers act after they have been forced to maim a book in order to get it (or most of it) into print, for writers who have felt dishonored earlier, during an expurgation, very rarely compound that shame by disowning a book after the publishers have kept their end of the bargain. To repudiate a published book is to dishonor a business deal, as well as a nearly sure-fire way to lose a publisher and warn off other publishers. We have almost no reason to conclude that Crane ever thought with shame of the pattern that was emerging – abject capitulation to Copeland and Day the year before and now, during the initial reception of *The Black Riders*, new accommodations to Hitchcock's suggestions. A book is a book, minus a little ethical sense and anarchy or not. At last, one of his pile of unpublished works was out in the world and being reviewed. Crane was ecstatic. In early June he expansively asked Copeland and Day to send him reviews and responded to a query of theirs with suggestions about various possible works of his that they might publish. They had apparently asked to see *Maggie*, but Crane did not have a copy at hand. Then they asked to see what he called his "eight little grotesque tales of the woods," and Crane asked for copies from the only person he knew who had them. Nothing came of this eager, free-wheeling spate of publishing schemes.

While all this was going on, *The Red Badge of Courage* was stalled. The question is why it was not published sooner if in fact Appleton had electroplated it in the spring. Crane presumably checked in with Hitchcock promptly after he returned in May, although he did not sign the Appleton contract until June 17 – a formality, since he had agreed to Hitchcock's terms by letter. As we have seen, in 1896 Hitchcock blamed the delay on Crane's absence when the proofs were ready. The delay was probably Hitchcock's, and it was probably strategic, for purposes that had nothing to do with the publishing seasons. He had a habit of getting his way when he wanted changes made, but getting his way in his own good time. Henry Binder has reminded us that in his 1900 introduction to *The Red Badge of Courage* Hitchcock twice repeated his 1896 claim that the delay was caused by proofreading. Citing the letter of January 6, 1896, in which Hitchcock made it clear that he was going to require revisions in *The Third Violet* even though he couched the delay as a desire to allow "plenty of time for the proof reading," Binder concluded that " 'proofreading' was a term the editor used to cover all operations he found necessary between the time a book was accepted and the time the final type was set – including the negotiating and carrying out of his own suggestions for revision." Certainly, proofreading the war story would have taken little time, and prompt publication would have allowed Appleton to capitalize on the sensation created by *The Black Riders*. And as Binder has pointed out, Hitchcock seems to have been an exemplary diplomat even though he routinely took extreme liberties as editor, as when he cut, rearranged, and rewrote the late Edward Noyes Westcott's *David Harum* and condensed Theodore Dreiser's *Jennie Gerhardt*. Comparatively speaking, he was taking few liberties with *The Red Badge of Courage* and, later, with *Maggie*.

What little documentary evidence survives besides the nature of the excisions – the worry about the title, the delays, the perplexing lie about the date of acceptance – all suggests that Hitchcock was taken aback when he saw the full manuscript of *The Red Badge of Courage*. He was apparently not perturbed about the stylistic oddities, for he knew that readers of the newspaper excerpts had been dazzled by Crane's originality of style. His initial concern seems to have been for the meaning, particularly as expressed in Chapter 12. He apparently did not immediately try to get Crane to rewrite (what Crane did in New Orleans seems to have been under his own impulses). On Crane's return, Hitchcock pressed first for the removal of the most explicit statements of the "ethical sense" of the book in the simplest way possible, by persuading Crane to make four simple cuts: the endings of Chapters 7, 10, and 15 and the entire Chapter 12. Binder is altogether convincing in positing a two-stage process for making the book fit for Appleton to print. The first is visible in the bound pages of the manuscript, for one can see the way the gaps were handled. When a whole page or more of text was to be omitted, Crane removed it and put bridge marks on the next page to be retained, so anyone making a typescript for the compositor to set from would know, for instance, that page 90 now followed page 85. (In this case, the whole of page 85 was retained for the sake of the top half, but the bottom half – the start of the offensive section – was marked through, although it remains legible.) Apparently Crane did the natural thing: He simply discarded the concluding pages of Chapter 7, 10, and 15, but he carried off with him all the pages of Chapter 12, since it was an intact unit (that four of the six pages survived his gypsy existence suggests that fairly soon they assumed some value in his eyes.)

Apparently Hitchcock was satisfied for the time being, or thought it politic to appear satisfied, since by June, Crane had the manuscript back and regarded it as disposable: As Binder shows, he gave four pages from Chapter 4 to his acquaintance William Jordan to serve as setting copy for an excerpt entitled "In the Heat of the Battle" in the August 1895 issue of *Current Literature*. (The compositor also did the natural thing and threw the pages away after setting from them.) Still later, apparently, Hitchcock negotiated the small cuts in the last chapter, for they are not marked out in the manuscript. Passages depicting Fleming's persistent selfishness and vainglorious self-delusion were excised simply with an eye to preventing the chapter from meaning what it had plainly meant, not with any attention to consistency of characterization. They were not even made with sufficient care to avoid grammatical confusions. At one point the text was left containing only one identifiable "matter," although "matters" were still referred to. A little later, the removal of the referent made it impossible to tell what "conviction" was specified in "With this conviction came a store of assurance." Readers, Hitchcock surely knew, would make sense enough of what they had left, particularly if a new ending could push them toward a belief that the youth was now a hero.

It was at this time, after the big cuts were made, after the manuscript was quite superseded, that Hitchcock prevailed upon Crane to compose a new and upbeat final paragraph: "Over the river a golden ray of sun came through the hosts of leaden rain clouds." As John T. Winterich said in 1951, this sentence "bears the unmistakable spoor of the editor" and "sounds like a concession to the send-the-audience-home-feeling-good school." With these last changes – maybe the little decisively placed addition was the last of all – Hitchcock had engineered disproportionately great changes in the apparent meaning of crucial passages. In the first stage of expurgation, he had purged the book of the passages likely to prove most objectionable, those where Henry Fleming indulged in vaingloriously adolescent ontological heroics; in the second, the mopping-up stage, he had purged it of those where Fleming displayed a heartlessly triumphant egotism.

Hitchcock got what he wanted, but even so he was apparently not confident enough to market the book as a bold new prose work by the much-talked-about reporter and poet. The Appleton flier, which he must have written, tells dealers to pitch the book to the veterans, a big market still and one that controlled a fair proportion of what we now refer to as the national disposable income. Within a few months of the publication of *The Red Badge of Courage* in its shortened, safer form, Crane was proclaimed the great new genius of the decade. Chances are that Hitchcock was right – that the contemporary audience could excuse oddities of grammar and diction or even enjoy them in a vivid study of the psychological vacillations of a young recruit who ran from battle and then learned, apparently, to be brave. Hitchcock must have left in his *Red Badge of Courage* about all the essential Crane his contemporaries could have stood. The Crane that Hitchcock saw fit to print was enough to create a literary sensation not only among journalists in Philadelphia but also among established writers of fiction such as Joseph Conrad and Henry James.

Crane probably did not often look back grievingly at what he had sacrificed from his war novel any more than he looked back at the ethical sense and anarchy he had sacrificed from *The Black Riders*. He did realize, a little belatedly, that what was left of the manuscript might have some value, so in January 1896 he bundled most of it up (he did not bother to find the pages of Chapter 12) and sent it to his friend Willis Brooks Hawkins with a studiedly laconic comment: "Thought maybe you'd like it." That Crane had some moments of uneasiness when he thought of his textual sacrifices may be deduced from his comments on Hitchcock in a letter to Nellie Crouse on January 6, 1896, while he was waiting for Hitchcock's response to the manuscript of *The Third Violet:* "When you said that Hitchcock mentioned me, I was alarmed for I thought you meant Ripley Hitchcock of New York and I knew just how he would mention anybody save himself and God. I resolved to overthrow him on the first opportunity. But then I perceived that you meant Hitchcock of Buffalo. His name, you understand, is Hitchy. If you had said that Hitchy mentioned me, I would have known at once." Crane was getting some of his work into print, albeit in truncated form, but when he thought about the situation, he was not exactly proud of what getting into print had cost him in artistic integrity.

Even the international acclaim that began to greet *The Red Badge of Courage* before the end of 1895 did not transform Hitchcock into an uncritical idolator of his young author. When he wrote Crane about *The Third Violet* on January 6, 1896, Hitchcock was polite but unenthusiastic: The novel needed work, and he wanted to see Crane in person, though it would require Crane to make a trip to town from Hartwood, in west central New York. Their meeting was inconclusive, and what happened next was at Hitchcock's initiative, not Crane's. Unwilling to publish the tepid *The Third Violet* as a follow-up to the extraordinary *The Red Badge of Courage,* and reflecting on his options after Crane returned to Hartwood, Hitchcock had a brainstorm. He did not have a copy of the 1893 edition of *Maggie,* but he had read the manuscript in 1892 or so, before rejecting it, and he remembered it well enough to know that now, in the aftermath of the success of the war novel, it could be salvaged – tamed down, but left remarkable in subject and style. Soon he had Crane at work dispensing "with a goodly number of damns" and otherwise plugging away "at the words which hurt." From the extraordinary length of time Crane took on this small chore, we can only infer that the expurgation was un-congenial to him, however pleased he was that *Maggie* (in its "new aspect") would have a chance for life.

This time, as I have said, there is no question that Hitchcock was right: Appleton could not have published the novel Crane had printed in 1893. Since the subject matter remained dangerous despite all the expurgations – readers spared the sight of the fat man would still know that Maggie became a prostitute – there was an additional reason for eliminating some of the extreme linguistic usages along with the swear words: If the subject matter by its nature was certain to offend some people, there was no use inviting objections to the style as well. However much structural damage the omission of the fat man caused to the Appleton *Maggie*, and however much originality of style was sacrificed throughout, the plain fact remains that the story did not seem pallid to its readers in 1896, and it did not seem pallid to later writers on Crane who did not know they were reading an expurgated text: John Berryman, for instance, wrote about *Maggie* in 1950 as showing crudity "in stylistic detail," but also "originality of conception" and other high virtues. Hitchcock was, after all, paid to be right about what the taste of his time would allow, and for many years he was conspicuously good at his job. By sanitizing *The Red Badge of Courage* and then *Maggie*, Hitchcock brilliantly orchestrated Crane's debut as a fiction writer. So what if he ensured that readers would not know that the title of *The Red Badge of Courage* was ironic? So what if Maggie's last encounter had been excised? Who needs ethical sense and anarchy? Crane was a famous young man until he died in 1900.

In the first years of this century, Crane's reputation dimmed somewhat. A collected edition in the 1920s made most of Crane's works available, but few people read more than the war novel and some of the poems. Throughout the 1930s, the 1893 *Maggie* was famous as a bibliographical rarity, not as a variant, unexpurgated text. After World War II, colleges and courses in American literature multiplied. The coincidental triumph of the New Criticism meant that short stories such as "The Open Boat" and "The Blue Hotel" could be taught apart from much biographical information. Explications of these two stories proliferated in the academic journals. In recent years, Crane critics have continued to ignore almost everything besides *The Red Badge of Courage, Maggie*, and a few favorite stories: You won't find *George's Mother* very often in the indexes to the volumes of *American Literary Scholarship*, even though Crane thought it left *Maggie* "at the post." Crane has been, all this time, a classic writer primarily on the basis of one book, *The Red Badge of Courage*, known in a slightly shortened form – a form in which the cuts have consequences out of proportion to their length.

When R. W. Stallman and others began to pay attention to the original text of *Maggie* in the 1950s, they quickly came to prefer it to the expurgated version that had been generally available. Almost no work had been done on this novel, so critics did not have any vested interest in defending an interpretation that had been lavished on an expurgated text. (It would be interesting to know if Berryman, one of the most brilliant readers of Crane, *ever* knew the 1893 *Maggie*.) Scholars were free to acknowledge the original version of the novel as an even stronger example of naturalism than anyone had suspected, and therefore a valuable document for their revisions of literary history. Joseph Katz celebrated it in 1966 as "The *Maggie* Nobody Knows," and Donald Pizer introduced a facsimile edition of the 1893 *Maggie* in 1968. Fredson Bowers's edition in 1969 (basically a tidied up reprint of the 1896 edition with a few of the hurtful 1893 words restored) brought Crane scholars and interested bystanders out in force against him, so that in 1980 Edwin H. Cady could make this pronouncement: "Like Donald Pizer, Joseph Katz, and Hershel Parker (and almost everybody else), I thought Bowers was wrong."

Through the 1960s, I had brought to my classes quotations from the manuscript of *The Red Badge of Courage* to show how anomalies arose in the last chapter. I did not quite bother to name what I was doing, but I was resorting to the manuscript because the last chapter did not make sense. In 1975 I belatedly put one and one, *Maggie* and *The Red Badge of Courage*, together and decided that the pattern should have been clear all along – Hitchcock got Crane to cut the war novel just as he got him to cut the slum novel a few months later. All I had been learning about the creative process through working with writers' drafts and revisions (and through studying the writing of aestheticians and psychologists) tended to show, as I have said, that the creative process is in fact a process, one that ends with such finality that rarely can any author return to a completed work and revise it in accordance with the plans he projected and the impulses he felt as he worked through to its completion. Still more rarely will a writer manage to revise a book coherently when he is being required to do so by an editor or publisher. And routinely, writers will agree to cuts without ever seeing even the grossest aesthetic damage those cuts do locally or elsewhere in the work. Knowing that authors do things or agree to things that damage the "authority" of their own texts, I was not inhibited by the fact that Crane had agreed to the cuts. I wanted to read it the way he wrote it.

Using Bowers's *Facsimile,* I read the manuscript, including what was left visible of the deleted chapter endings, and I supplemented the crossed-out passages with any earlier version in the surviving pages of the draft; when I finished Chapter 11, I read the surviving pages of Chapter 12 and supplemented them in the same way; and I read the full original last chapter, where nothing was crossed out because the chapter had survived the first phase of Hitchcock's expurgations. The few hours were a time of wonder and awe, for I was reading the book almost as Ripley Hitchcock had seen it, and as no one, apparently, had done since 1895, despite the gradual availability of the bound manuscript and scattered pages over the last three decades. Binder later pointed out that Bowers had made it extremely difficult to think in terms of what Crane wrote when he defined the "manuscript" as the pages that Crane gave Linson and relegated the surviving pages of Chapter 12 to a section in the back of the *Facsimile.* What I read was a great book and a coherent book, one that, from beginning to end, treated the young recruit with ironic objectivity. When I set about getting what Crane wrote into print as closely as it could be reconstructed, I did not expect the restored *The Red Badge of Courage* to create any more opposition than the 1893 edition of *Maggie* had done. Modern critics had written themselves into an impasse over the ending of the war novel, so they would be relieved to find that the reason they couldn't agree, despite their earnest explications, was not that they were merely a pack of notorious wranglers but that they were arguing about a partially unreadable text. I was naive, but I was also patient, and still am.

Readers will come round, I am hopeful. After all, in recent decades we have had to readjust often enough to a form of a classic text more unfamiliar even than the "new" *Maggie* or the "new" *The Red Badge of Courage.* Every student now knows a *Prelude* different from what Tennyson and Browning knew. We are now accustoming ourselves to a *Billy Budd, Sailor* that no longer begins with the "Preface" that the first editor supplied from what was in fact a discarded passage from a late chapter. We routinely avoid anachronisms when we talk about the texts that were available at a given time, recognizing that it matters that Conrad said what he said on the basis of a reprint of the Appleton edition of *The Red Badge of Courage*, just as it matters that D. H. Lawrence formed his opinions about *Moby-Dick* from a reprint of *The Whale* (one that lacked – for all of Lawrence's interest in the homoerotic elements – Ishmael and Queequeg's "hearts' honeymoon," during which Queequeg performs intimate motions with his "brown tattooed legs"). To be sure, critics blunder now and then, as when F. R. Leavis praised the astonishing maturity of Henry James's early style while quoting from the New York edition, the product of James's ripe maturity. Most of us, however, manage nicely to keep our historical senses alert in such cases, and it should not be especially difficult to accept *The Red Badge of Courage* in something very close to its original form. Now that the centennial of the publication approaches, we ought to be ready for a Stephen Crane with a little more ethical sense and anarchy and a lot more structural unity and cogency of characterization. Ironically enough, we have at last a text worth the most devoted attention from literary critics, after four decades of criticism have been misdevoted to an expurgated text. As I said at the end of *Flawed Texts and Verbal Icons*, "when you read the reconstructed *The Red Badge of Courage*, even though some of its crimson paint and gold leaf has been battered off irreparably, you hold what's left of an authentic textual icon."

I have worded this essay so as to obviate notes. Always, Crane's letters are from *Stephen Crane: Letters*, ed. R. W. Stallman and Lillian Gilkes (New York: New York University Press, 1960). References to events in Crane's life are from Stallman's *Stephen Crane: A Biography* (New York: George Braziller, 1968; rev., 1973). Stallman's *Stephen Crane: A Critical Bibliography* (Ames: Iowa State University Press, 1972) is badly organized (for instance, within a given year, reviews of *The Red Badge of Courage* are listed not chronologically but alphabetically by name of periodical); because important facts are buried at odd places, anyone interested in Crane must read it as if it were narrative. (Page 101 is my source for the Appleton public notice in the *New York Times* on April 3, 1896.) All my quotations from the draft of *The Red Badge of Courage* and from the final manuscript are from *The Red Badge of Courage: A Facsimile Edition of the*

Manuscript, ed. Fredson Bowers (Washington: NCR/Microcard Editions, 1973). The 1894 newspaper excerpts from the novel are available in *''The Red Badge of Courage'' by Stephen Crane: A Facsimile Reproduction of the New York ''Press'' Appearance of December 9, 1894,* intro. Joseph Katz (Gainesville, Fla.: Scholars' Facsimiles & Reprints, 1967).

Here I specify the sources for a few allusions that might otherwise prove elusive. The Appleton flier (the dealers' order form for *The Red Badge of Courage*) is reproduced as the frontispiece to the special Crane issue of *Studies in the Novel* 10 (Spring 1978). The Copeland and Day letters to Crane are in Joseph Katz's introduction to *The Complete Poems of Stephen Crane.* Ripley Hitchcock's letter to Crane on January 6, 1896, is from Henry Binder's lead essay in the 1978 Crane issue of *Studies in the Novel,* p. 46, fn. 33, and is reprinted in Binder's expansion of this essay in *The Red Badge of Courage* (New York: W. W. Norton, 1982), p. 156, fn. 33. For this Norton version, Binder added some comments on Hitchcock as editor of Edward Noyes Westcott and Theodore Dreiser (pp. 126–7). Binder analyzed the textual significance of the *Current Literature* excerpt in ''Unwinding the Riddle of Four Pages Missing from the *Red Badge of Courage* Manuscript,'' *PBSA* 72 (1978):100–6.

3

The American Stephen Crane: The Context of *The Red Badge of Courage*

ANDREW DELBANCO

Culture, in its true sense, I take it, is a comprehension of the man at
one's shoulder.
                                    −Stephen Crane to Willis Brooks Hawkins, 1895

W RITING in 1866, in the doomed, sad language of Lincoln's
Second Inaugural Address, Herman Melville counseled his
countrymen on how to think about the Civil War that had just
ended: "Noble was the gesture into which patriotic passion surprised the people in a utilitarian time and country; yet the glory of
the war falls short of its pathos − a pathos which now at last ought
to disarm all animosity." Melville wanted Americans to face what
had happened to them, to recognize at what cost they had spent
their blood and store − but he was not quite willing to say, in
retrospective chastisement, that they had brought the catastrophe
upon themselves. "Perhaps," he conceded, "nothing could have
averted the strife, and . . . to treat of human actions is to deal
wholly with second causes." Into this sentence there crept the idea
of necessity: the notion that all the Bible-thumping abolitionists,
and Free Soilers, and Conscience Whigs, and Southern nullifica-
tionists, indeed all who had thought themselves self-motivated
actors in the years that led to war − had been caught in a collective
delusion about their freedom to act and to control the results of
their actions. Behind the reasoning debators and the irrational
mobs, the committed slave smugglers who brought fugitives north
and the bounty hunters who returned them south, and finally,
behind the two great armies that threw themselves at each other
for four years, there lay − Melville was suggesting − an invisible
First Cause. This was something that used to be called God, or, by
some who preferred a more secular language, history. But by the

time Melville collected his *Battle-Pieces* in 1866, a dead generation was covering the earth, as Scott Fitzgerald was to say of the victims of a later war, "like a million bloody rugs" – and so the question arose of whether the God of history who had foreknowingly laid them there could any longer have a pronounceable name.[1]

The event itself had been given a name before it began. It was, said Senator (later Secretary of State) William H. Seward in 1858, "an irrepressible conflict," a phrase, as Kenneth Stampp has argued, that has set the terms of debate over the causes of the Civil War ever since. However powerfully some recent historians have made the case that the war was a miserable political accident, to those who witnessed its approach it was a conflict both "irrepressible" and of cosmic proportions. Orators on both sides fixed on Milton as their ideal "War-Laureate," in whose "Manichean imagery" they discerned the outline of the national crisis. Some even saw in Jefferson Davis a latter-day version of Milton's Satan, whom James Russell Lowell described as "the first great secessionist." There were, of course, bitterly conflicting claims about God's allegiance in war-divided America, but there was little acknowledged doubt on either side (at least not in public discourse) about his *involvement*. During the war, it was simply unthinkable that God might have been indifferent to the purposes and outcome of the nation's bloodletting. By the end of the war, this had become a thought that needed to be kept at bay.[2]

And so, it is not surprising that when the fighting was over and American writers undertook what Edmund Wilson has called the "chastening of American prose style" – the reduction of metaphoric density to the spare language of realism – the organ tones of union oratory became more often a subject for parody than for celebration. For one thing, the permissible limits of parody had expanded: Novelists like Edward Eggleston, William Dean Howells, and Harold Frederic even began to ridicule the pretensions of the droning clergy, and Mark Twain delivered a notorious speech on the occasion of John Greenleaf Whittier's seventieth birthday in 1877, a performance that left the New England clerisy in a "petrified condition," as if Twain had "been making those remarks about the Deity and the rest of the Trinity." The new literary iconoclasm was nowhere more bitterly expressed than by those writers (in this case, J. W. DeForest) who took the war itself as their subject and wrote about it in sentences that seem too weary to go on for long:

> I had just finished breakfast, and was lying on my back smoking. A bullet whistled so unusually low as to attract my attention and struck with a loud smash in a tree about twenty feet from me. Between me and the tree a soldier with his greatcoat rolled under his head for a pillow lay on his back reading a newspaper which he held in both hands. I remember smiling to myself to see this man start as the bullet passed. Some of his comrades left off playing cards and looked for it. The man who was reading remained perfectly still, his eyes fixed on the paper with a steadiness which I thought curious, considering the bustle around him. Presently I noticed that there were a few drops of blood on his neck, and that his face was paling. Calling to the card players, who had resumed their game, I said, "See to that man with the paper." They went to him, spoke to him, touched him, and found him perfectly dead. The ball had struck him under the chin, traversed the neck, and cut the spinal column where it joins the brain, making a fearful hole through which the blood had already soaked his greatcoat. It was this man's head and not the tree which had been struck with such a report. There he lay, still holding the New York *Independent*, with his eyes fixed on a sermon by Henry Ward Beecher. It was really quite a remarkable circumstance.

Beecher's sermon was doubtless concerned chiefly with what President Buchanan, using the prewar rhetoric of moderation, had called "superintending providence."[3] That precious participle carried the assurance that the divine will could absorb into itself the small, changeable intentions of men. When DeForest reduced this idea of superintendence to a macabre joke in his ironically titled novel, *Miss Ravenel's Conversion from Secession to Loyalty* (1867), he was writing against a concept that was still alive. His book belongs, with Hemingway's *The Sun Also Rises* (1926) and Mailer's *The Naked and the Dead* (1948), to that category of immediately post-war fiction — books that call Pyrrhic a victory whose celebrations have barely passed.

1

With such a lineage in mind, it becomes more than a curiosity that the most famous of all American war novels was written thirty-five years after the Civil War began by a man who had not yet been born when it ended. If DeForest and Ambrose Bierce had known firsthand how it sounded when a bullet pierced a human skull, Stephen Crane's closest taste of war before he wrote *The Red Badge* was at Claverack College, a military school on the east bank of the Hudson, where he drilled with his classmates and marched about the playing fields in adolescent self-delight. Crane had, of course, not "remained [entirely] deaf to the echoes" of the Civil War, a national noise that has been summarized as "memoirs, biographies, regimental histories, multivolumed chronicles, pamphlets, poems, diaries," and the voices of "veterans more than ready to reminisce about the most exciting years of their lives." But despite Crane's secondhand education, more than a few readers were fooled into thinking that *The Red Badge* was a firsthand account of combat. One Civil War veteran was startlingly sure: "I was with Crane at Antietam."[4]

The Red Badge, in short, seemed authentic in ways that other writers in Crane's time, notably Hamlin Garland, insisted could come only from personal experience. Not every reviewer was equally persuaded that the young author had actually seen war, but contemporary reaction to his novel was nearly unanimous in judging it an astonishing success at drawing the reader into an intimacy with battle. Crane was fortunate in his reviewers – both in their praise and their insight. One anonymous critic for the New York *Press*, for example, provided as good a summary comment as any since: "The description is so vivid as to be almost suffocating. The reader is right down in the midst of it where patriotism is dissolved into its elements and where only a dozen men can be seen, firing blindly and grotesquely into the smoke. This is war from a new point of view, and it seems more real than when seen with an eye only for large movements and general effects."[5] This reader grasped what more recent critics have elaborated at length: that Crane, like his impressionist painter contemporaries, avoided the use of illusionist techniques (in the case of painting, this meant, for example, perspective and line outlining; in the case of prose fiction, it meant supplying an ideological context, e.g., North versus South in a war of slave liberation, as a frame for scene and event). If Sisley and Monet, without recourse to the traditional visual vocabulary of Western painting, strove for accuracy in replicating the pure experience of the eye, Crane similarly refused to provide a conceptual context for purely sensory experience. His book seems utterly devoid of political ideas – so much so that one recent critic (making an implicit appeal to the currently favored notion of "absence" as an element of meaning in literary texts), has suggested that Crane left political comment out of *The Red Badge* precisely in order to create a kind of pestering void.[6] By ignoring the political dimension of the conflict, Crane was, according to this view, deliberately affronting the emotion of American nationalism for which the Civil War remained, in 1895, the formative symbol. Crane's earliest reviewers, it should be acknowledged, knew this: They knew that in writing about "war from a new point of view," he was eschewing the grand perspective, say, of Tolstoy in *War and Peace* (1869). The question has never been whether this is so; the question remains, however, why did Crane make it so?

Using his own preferred sort of organic metaphor, we may say that Crane was pressing the palm so close against the reader's face that only its creases and pores could be discerned, never its function as part of hand, or limb, or body. In Crane's fictive world, the senses admit smell and color and shape – fractional impressions from which one can only guess at the meaning of the whole – or indeed, whether there is any meaning to the whole at all:

> Into the nostrils came a subtly strong odor of powder-smoke, oil, wet earth. . . . Our guide strode abruptly into the gloom. His lamp flared shades of yellow and orange upon the walls of a tunnel. . . . Little points of coal caught the light and shone like diamonds.[7]

This is Crane's description (in an 1894 *McClure's* feature) of a coal mine – a piece that becomes a purely aesthetic meditation, evoking the drop of the elevator into the shaft, the crunch of shoes on the coal dust, and thereby taunting the reader's expectation that it will proceed with a muckraker's rage. Crane's Civil War novel undercuts the reader's expectation in much the same way; it robs the engagement of all specificity and refuses to situate it within a large conflict, making the "battle a type and nam[ing] no names."[8] It seeks thereby to replicate as closely as possible the experience of war for the sensate individual, for whom large historical forces were at an invisible distance. As part of his fidelity to felt experience, Crane [like Stanley Kubrick in his great war film, *Paths of Glory* (1957)] leaves the enemy virtually unseen, glimpsed only briefly as "machines of steel" or as a faceless "brown swarm." We are given a sense of war as an experience entirely devoid of the engagement of the will, with no aim whatever in the combatants' minds – neither tactical nor political – except to survive. This is something that Fleming himself at least partly understands: "the swift thought came to him that the generals did not know what they were about." On Crane's battlefield the sole and constant concern is survival: "you've got t' hold 'em back," shouts a hatless general as the rebel swarm threatens to pour over the defenders' line, "you've got t'hold 'em back." Resistance means everything in the world of *The Red Badge;* nothing save rumor originates in the minds of the soldiers, who are purely reactive creatures. If the sound and sight of the flapping flag – "sun-touched, resplendent" – are sometimes huge in Henry Fleming's consciousness, the socially inscribed meaning of the flag is an abstraction quite outside his understanding, and becomes equally so for us. Reading *The Red Badge* relieves us of our ideology and, to the extent that this is ever possible, replaces it with raw experience.

Some of this is well known, perhaps too well known – for it has fostered a sense that Crane's "impressionistic" treatment of the war was tantamount to his regarding it as an event outside history. Crane, we are repeatedly told, made use of his historical material (the battle conforms fairly closely to the events at Chancellorsville in 1863) solely for the purpose of making a psychological demonstration. He had, in John Berryman's words, "no interest in the causes, meaning, or outcome of the war," a proposition that Alfred Kazin not only confirms but amplifies: "He cared not a jot which way the world went." Daniel Aaron, advisedly using the language of performance, adds detail to the indictment: "Negroes and Lincoln and hospitals and prisons are not to be found in Crane's theater." Crane, it seems, was simply indifferent to historical and political questions; he was writing in full accord with Hamlin Garland's dictum that "the past is dead, and the future can be trusted to look after itself."[9]

The fact is, however, that such notions, put forward by persuasive readers in a variety of forms, have been stumbling blocks for modern Crane criticism. They represent a problem that grows more urgent as "the living chain of connection with the Civil War era is dissolving[,] as the last generation to know living voices from that time grows old."[10] With the war receding into a history accessible only through books, we have come to underestimate the possibility that Stephen Crane really did relive its trauma for his first readers, that he touched a nerve because he grasped the ways in which this particular war remained central, in 1895, to many who remembered it. We have lost touch with Stephen Crane's audience – and thereby, to some extent, with him.

Thirty years ago, Bernard Weisberger sensed this estrangement. He argued strenuously (but without much effect on subsequent critical opinion) that *The Red Badge of Courage* was "specifically an epic of America's national tragedy," that it was acutely sensitive to the particular trauma inflicted by the Civil War upon an "especially innocent" generation of country-bred boys who lived, until war threw them together, in the "unimaginable isolation" of rural America.[11] To those in that generation who survived (to become a part of Crane's reading public in the 1890s), one of the most convincing aspects of this Civil War novel was surely the permanent elusiveness of the enemy – not merely because he had sometimes seemed a wily guerrilla adept at concealment but also because he had been, and remained, fundamentally incomprehensible within the context of a single American nation:

> Various veterans had told him tales. Some talked of grey, be-whiskered hordes who were advancing, with relentless curses and chewing tobacco with unspeakable valor; tremendous bodies of fierce soldiery who were sweeping along like the Huns. Others spoke of tattered and eternally-hungry men who fired despondent powder. "They'll charge through hell's-fire an' brimstone t' git a holt on a haversack, an' sech stomachs aint a-lastin' long," he was told. From the stories, the youth imagined the red, live bones sticking out through slits in the faded uniforms.

> However, he perceived now that it did not greatly matter what kind of soldiers he was going to fight, so long as they fought, which fact no one disputed. There was a more serious problem. He lay in

his bunk pondering upon it. He tried to mathematically prove to himself that he would not run from a battle. (Chap. 1)

There is a submerged but clearly causal relation between the first of these paragraphs and the second. Crane is hinting that Fleming's bewilderment over the nature of his enemy bears directly on his impulse to flee and that Fleming, moreover, knows this. He asks, nearly begs, for purpose:

> "Ma, I've enlisted," he had said to [his mother] diffidently.
> There was a short silence. "Th' Lord's will be done, Henry," she had finally replied and had then continued to milk the brindle cow.
> When he had stood in the door-way with his soldier's clothes on his back and with the light of excitement and expectancy in his eyes almost defeating the glow of regret for home bonds, he had seen two tears leaving their hot trails on his mother's scarred cheeks.
> Still, she had disappointed him by saying nothing whatever about returning with his shield or on it. (Chap. 1)

She disappoints him because she gives no blessing: "I don't know what else t' tell yeh."

The question here is not whether Stephen Crane was accurate in proposing that a generation of American boys went to war in the 1860s in bewilderment. The point is that Crane himself was not merely reporting but was *participating* in Henry's beseeching. His often-noted identification with Fleming – "the obscure forces," says Kazin, that ". . . suddenly drove him to write *The Red Badge* in ten continuous nights must have resembled the unrelenting pressure of battle" – began for him before the fictive battle. It began with the question of purpose, here expressed in an 1896 letter to Nellie Crouse:

> Upon my soul I have lost all appetite for victory, as victory is defined by the mob. I will be glad if I can feel on my death-bed that my life has been just and kind according to my ability and that every particle of my little ridiculous stock of eloquence and wisdom has been applied for the benefit of my kind. . . . I do not even expect to do good. But I expect to make a sincere, desperate, lonely battle to remain true to my conception of life and the way it should be lived, and if this plan can accomplish anything, it shall be accomplished. It is not a fine prospect. I only speak of it to people in whose opinions I have faith.[12]

Crane's voice here is characteristically mixed in the service of self-aggrandizement, charity, faith, militance, fatalism – the voice of a man who was in limbo all his life between his own disinterested generation that came of age in the Darwinian 1890s and the generation represented by his parents, both of whom had taken part in the reform and political activism of an earlier day. If the character and destiny of American nationhood eluded him as the issues at stake in the Civil War, then, in the end, he felt their absence not as a means to taunt naive believers, but as the loss of an immensely valuable act of mind.

Stephen Crane wrote *The Red Badge* out of and about a crisis of faith – both about God and about God's instrument, the American nation. He wrote it, furthermore, with a sense of disorientation in which the idea of purposeful sacrifice seemed irrecoverable. His fiction, despite all its gestures of irreverence toward naive notions of heroism, is cast in the mode of lamentation for a bygone day of moral clarity. This elegiac mood is perhaps most delicately achieved in such minor sketches from the early 1890s as ''Mr. Binks' Day Off'' and ''The Broken-Down Van'' (both about the city man's craving for pastoral peace) or in the Melvillean meditation on ''The Art Students' League Building.'' It is clearest, if a bit forced, in the short story that Crane wrote in 1896 as a kind of appendix to *The Red Badge*, ''The Veteran'' – a portrait of Henry Fleming in heroic old age, written utterly without the ironic understatement that we think of as Crane's stylistic legacy in American letters as it descended through Hemingway to the early Mailer. But it is present in *The Red Badge* as well, which is less a book of scorn toward men deluded than a book of yearning for something better than delusion. When Crane describes Fleming's redeemer fantasies, for example, he speaks with a more than gentle doubt, but with a less than Biercean contempt: ''He had, presently, a feeling that he was the growing prophet of a world-reconstruction. . . . He conceived a new world modelled by the pain of his life, and in which no old shadows fell blighting upon the temple of thought. And there were many personal advantages to it'' (Chap. 12). There is always more pain than triumph in Crane's skepticism, even as he remarks on the egoism of Fleming's dream of ''world-reconstruction'': ''As the youth looked at [his fellow soldiers advancing to the front], the black weight of his woe returned to him. He felt that he was regarding a procession of chosen beings. The separation was as great to him as if they had marched with weapons of flame and banners of sun-light. He could never be like them. He could have wept in his longings" (Chap. 11). For Fleming this separation between the church militant and the excluded witness signifies, first of all, a failure of character. But for Crane it was also a failure to be generalized into a picture of manifold slippage in American life.

That picture is a composite that can be assembled out of the separable concerns of Crane's works. The once contested issue of race, for instance, is powerfully present even in his unfinished novel, *The O'Ruddy* (1903) – a book about a man of colonial mentality (nominally a high-spirited Irishman of open character and no duplicity) who finds himself in ritual-crazed England, where men "salaam one to another and mouth out fool-phrases and cavort and prance and caracole until I thought them mad." In the romance tradition of Hawthorne and Twain, *The O'Ruddy* is a book of no real geographic fixity, but it is emphatically about an Old World problem – the replacement of one man's original identity by the status-conscious mentality of his "betters." Through a series of complicated developments that eventually leave him scrambling for a living as a highwayman, he is wrested into a kind of doppelgänger relation to a black man, with whom he duels his way to a new sense of self. There is the shimmer of allegory in this plot that converts a natural-mannered colonial into a grasping master at war with the black subordinate. It may even be a displaced version of the tale Crane would have written in his aborted novel of the American Revolution – a tale of America's moral history as a struggle against European habits of mind. ("Read Fenimore Cooper's *Spy*,"[13] he had instructed himself as he worked up his material for the book he never wrote – a book that, like Cooper's, might have turned out to be less about the achievement of home rule than about the fate of those who ruled at home.) In any case, the cackling bystanders in his "Irish" novel egg on the white and black combatants whom they have stirred into enmity.

Several critics, notably Ralph Ellison, have recognized that what is oblique in *The O'Ruddy* is clear in Crane's great story of 1899,

"The Monster": "Behind the non-committal mask of [Crane's] prose," writes Ellison, there is "a conviction that man exists . . . at the mercy of . . . his own misconceptions." The leading misconception in "The Monster" is of course a racist one – the terrible disfigurement that the black man, Johnson, suffers as he saves a white child from death by fire only confirms his monstrosity in the eyes of the observing white world. These works are not productions of a socially indifferent mind. They reflect an insolent independence on questions of race (an independence especially notable in the 1890s, which was a time of severe retrenchment for the rights and dignity of black people in America). Crane was not so much seeking "to puncture some overgrown pieties about American 'idealism' in fighting the civil war" as to find reasons to be pious about America. His dissent from the mood of the 1890s was, moreover, not lost on his contemporaries; Teddy Roosevelt, for instance, responded this way to one of Crane's tales of a gunfight between westerners and a group of Mexican bandits: "Some day I want you to write another story of the frontiersman and the Mexican Greaser in which the frontiersman shall come out on top; it is more normal that way!"[14]

If we think, then, about Crane as a writer who had devastating things to say about American notions of "normalcy," it becomes possible to understand why at the very end of his life he became almost frantically interested in the history of America's creation, especially in the role played by his fellow New Jerseyans in the war for independence. Beginning to sense, in J. C. Levenson's phrase, "his deep implication in a continuum of past and present," he scrambled for books that might help him compose a coherent statement about the birth of American identity. In his tubercular frailty, he dictated to Cora a note of self-instruction that includes such assignments as this: "Find out if Lord Chatams speeches were known in colonies soon after deliverance." Crane was beginning to develop a genuinely sophisticated sense of the complexity of the American past: "Point out in some way that americans were excessively willing to meet the British in pitch battles wheras that was not their best policy at all. [A better] policy was to make guerilla warfare; vide the cubans [but] on second thoughts [an American home tended to be] a house; not a hut and if the inhabitants fled from it to the hills or wood they left behind them considerable material property. Introduce Henry Flemings grandfather as first farmer."[15] There is in these jottings a matured sense of how difficult and serious a task it is to recover the full experience of past lives; and more particularly, an instinct that the story of American independence has to do with the shedding of European habits of mind that had become liabilities in the New World. This sort of historical recovery, as Weisberger suggested, is at least part of what Crane was after in *The Red Badge*. The fact that few recent critics have agreed says more about the limits of Crane's success than about his intention.

Through all his efforts to make such a recovery, Crane remained obsessed (especially in his many works on war) with the theme of the undamaged observer who is "not able," as the narrator says in *The Third Violet* (1897), "to see things with a true eye." He knew from his own professional experience that the writer in America depended for his livelihood not on a true eye but on a sharp eye for what sold. Indeed, his own concessions in revising the manuscript of *The Red Badge* for the Appleton edition – most famously, the addition of the final sunshine sentence, "Over the river a golden ray of sun came through the host of leaden rain clouds" – may have been made with what we nowadays call "viewer tolerance" in mind, a compromise that surely left him wondering whether he was sugaring his subject for public consumption. The theme of pandering to the customers' prurience explodes more bitterly in *Active Service* (1899), a book whose personal bearing is barely disguised (the leading female character is named Nora – close enough to Cora to make the portrait nastily clear). *Active Service* is a book about what Henry James had called a "publishing scoundrel," a man who will do anything to please his readership:

> There had been a babe with no arms born in one of the western counties of Massachusetts. In place of upper limbs the child had growing from its chest a pair of fin-like hands, mere bits of skin covered bones. Furthermore it had only one eye. This phenomenon lived four days but the news of the birth had travelled up this country-road and through that village until it had reached the ears of the editor of the *Michaelstown Tribune*. He was also a correspondent for the *New York Eclipse*. On the third day he appeared at the home of the parents accompanied by a photographer. While the

latter arranged his instrument, the correspondent talked to the father and mother, two cow-eyed and yellow-faced people who
seemed to suffer a primitive fright of the strangers. Afterward as the
correspondent and the photographer were climbing into their buggy, the mother crept furtively down to the gate and asked, in a
foreigner's dialect, if they would send her a copy of the photograph.
The correspondent, carelessly indulgent, promised it. As the buggy
swung away, the father came from behind an apple-tree and the
two semi-humans watched it with its burden of glorious strangers
until it rumbled across the bridge and disappeared. The correspondent was elate; he told the photographer that the *Eclipse* would
probably pay fifty dollars for the article and the photograph.
(Chap. 3)

This lacerating self-contempt holds a clue to the mood in which
Crane always wrote about war (*Active Service* goes on to expose the
journalist as a man who makes private use of "the celebration of
the [Greek] people . . . even as in the theater, the music accom-
panies the hero in his progress").

The Red Badge represents no exception to this mood. Crane understood well the sheepishness of the voyeur who peers with deli-
cious release at what Arthur Miller calls "the man whose death
leaves you relieved that you are not him." He felt, in short, guiltily
excused from history's determinative moments – even as he felt
compelled to observe and record them. There is in Crane a Haw-
thornian embarrassment before his activist fathers and, despite his
craving for approval, a contempt for the audience that bought his
wares. Here, for example, he ponders on the ancestor after whom
he was named and imagines him at the center of his aborted novel
of the Revolution: "Picture of marching British army as it passed
Stephen Crane's house, where he lay dying."[16] This eighteenth-
century Stephen Crane was a witness, not a voyeur well paid for
his dispatches – and his descendant knew it.

2

Perhaps the leading reason for Crane's growing sensitivity to missed
social obligation and to disconnection from his own heritage of
political engagement was the fact that his father, Jonathan Towneley Crane, had been a passionate Unionist. In fact, the Reverend J.

T. Crane had been a clergyman who wrote precisely the sort of sermon upon which DeForest fixed the eyes of his dead soldier. We still know this father mostly in caricature – as a man full of disapproval, whose face, stiffly posed for the daguerrotypist, is pinched behind his pince-nez. And we still tend to think of his disheveled son as a proud opposite, sporting outrageous cravats, smoking, with exhibitionistic delight, his hookah. There is, of course, some basis for this picture. "A whole generation of young people," wrote Stephen's stern-visaged father, "are growing up, to whom solid books are unknown, to whom the great historic names of the past are but a sound, and whose ignorance of the world of fact is poorly compensated by their acquaintance with the world of dreams."[17] Though he was not yet born when those words were written, Stephen has been regarded as just such an unlettered boy, "virtually without a knowledge of the past," an eager conscript in the philistine generation that his father abhorred. It is perfectly true that Crane – if he is placed beside his bookish contemporaries James and Howells – seems an untutored and undisciplined talent, a kind of idiot savant. A few critics, however, have rightly cautioned that though "he had thrown off religion, his religious inheritance survived," and, as Joseph Katz has recently remarked, it is important to recognize that his family "lived by the word – by reading, writing, and speaking it . . . and [that] from the cradle Crane absorbed their knowledge."[18] (Henry Binder has usefully called attention in his edition of *The Red Badge* to its many "vestiges of Biblical imagery.") Crane, then, carried his family with him much longer and more reverently than we have sometimes supposed; his personal library included not only such tracts as his uncle Jesse Peck's *What must I do to be Saved?* (1858) and John Williams' *Pastoral Letter from a minister to his parishioners, being an earnest exhortation to them to take care of their souls* (1700), but also a copy of George Bancroft's providential *History of the United States* (1838). These books did not hold their place on his shelf merely as material for amused rejection. Crane's well-known remark that his father (and "everybody" on his mother's side) was of the "ambling-nag, saddle-bag" school of preaching was surely as much a boisterous expression of adolescent embarrassment as a serious commentary on his heritage. Realizing this, Daniel Hoffman has pointed to the inscription that Crane placed in his gift copies of *Maggie* – "environment is a tremendous thing in the world and shapes lives regardless" – and suggested that even as he handed out copies of his most naturalistic book, Crane could not entirely suppress the language of salvation: "If one proves that theory [of environmentalism], one makes room in Heaven for all sorts of souls."[19] It may be added that even if one speaks (as does Daniel Aaron) only ironically of Fleming's head gash as his "bloody sign of election," one may still detect a homiletic impulse beneath Crane's "short, sharp sentences hurled without sequence."[20] Crane the iconoclast is convincing, but Crane the nonbeliever is not. He is, to be sure, full of revulsion for gestures of sham piety, but he is never wholly free from the appetite for the very idea of divine superintendence that the Civil War had thrown into doubt and, more seriously, into disrepute. At the moment when Fleming shakes his fist at the sky and begins his "phillipic" (Chapter 9), or when he wanders into the wooded place "where the high, arching boughs made a chapel" and "a religious half light" illuminates the sight of ravenous ants nibbling on a dead man (Chapter 7), the writing is suffused with the kind of indignation that comes not from indifference to belief but from outrage at the betrayal of belief. At moments like this, Crane is a version of Saul Bellow's "atheist" Jew:

> What had made him an atheist was a massacre of Jews in his town. From the cellar where he was hidden he saw a laborer pissing on the body of his wife's younger brother, just killed. "So don't talk to me about God," he said. But it was he that talked about God, all the time.[21]

Despite his relatively unbuffetted childhood, Stephen Crane somehow knew better than any American writer since Melville and Twain how experience can sear the soul's convictions, and he coupled that knowledge with an equal awareness of the absurd inadequacy of inherited religion. Faith has to be an affair of the self, not of the fathers – and the corollary of Crane's contempt for those who claimed it lightly was his desire to experience it deeply for himself. The historical event that fused these insights into one for Crane was the American Civil War, which he treated in a novel that is, among other things, a brilliant demonstration of how language itself manifests the human appetite for belief:

The ranks opened covertly to avoid the corpse. The invulnerable dead man forced a way for himself. The youth looked keenly at the ashen face. The wind raised the tawny beard. It moved as if a hand were stroking it. (Chap. 3)

These sentences (more clipped, even, than DeForest's) are descriptions not of external reality but of a habit of mind that postulates, in the very act of perceiving, the roughly Christian sentiments that there is life in death and tenderness in nature. Between the "forced" of the second sentence and the "as if" of the fifth, there is a vacillation between metaphor and simile – alternatives between which the whole book wavers. At one moment, dying soldiers drop "like bundles," a similitude that maintains, if only barely, some distinction between men and garbage. At the next moment, however, the fallen soldiers are no longer *like* debris, they simply *are* debris. Crane, in short, was aware of language as an unchosen human possession that generates rather than merely records meaning. "The youth had been taught that a man became another thing in a battle. He saw his salvation in such a change." The operative word here is "thing," a word whose career in *The Red Badge* extends far beyond this sentence and carries with it the irony of its manifold aptness. "The youth had been taught" that men are elevated by war; he discovers, on the contrary, that they are debased. Crane was aware (as he makes clearest in "The Veteran") that the language with which Americans spoke and thought about their Civil War had not been and could never be entirely drained of signifying power. *The Red Badge of Courage* was, perhaps, written to bring that language closer to neutrality, but at the same time it demonstrated powerfully that there can never be such a thing as neutral description. Everything that Henry Fleming sees is rendered meaningful by his imagination; indeed, the *The Red Badge* is a perfectly sustained illustration of modernist (and, by now, conventional) relativism – here summarized by David Bleich: "An observer is a subject, and his means of perception define the essence of the object. . . . Knowledge is not a parent, a spouse, or a God; it is the subjective construction of our minds, which are more accessible to us than anything else."[22] In *The Red Badge* the flag, the sun, and the head gash are signs no longer to be read according to terms set by an earlier generation of interpreters, and though

Crane is merciless in exposing what may seem to us Fleming's "misreadings," he is at the same time frightened by the prospect of genuine relativism: "The artillery booming, forward, rearward, and on the flanks made jumble of ideas of direction. Landmarks had vanished into the gathering gloom." These are more than the landmarks of the local terrain. The Civil War battlefield was for Crane's Fleming what abandonment in the ocean had been for Pip in Melville's *Moby-Dick;* what the sight of Osmond and Merle had been for Isabel Archer in James's *The Portrait of a Lady;* what a ride on the Third Avenue El had been for Basil March in Howells's *A Hazard of New Fortunes.* It was an experience that obliterates all inherited points of moral and even perceptual reference.

Bearing this in mind, it may be fairly said that to preserve the gift of a common (Christian) language had been, for Stephen Crane's father, the definition of virtue, and that the unanchored life of the skeptical bystander had been his definition of sin. He was, it needs to be stressed, not merely a dutiful suburban preacher but a committed soldier in the ranks of the Northern Methodist Episcopal Church – an activist church that bridged the Finneyite evangelicalism of the early nineteenth century and the Social Gospel of the late. He was a man who, long before the Civil War began, wrote vigorously in support of black suffrage; who, when the fighting broke out, "ardently labored for the Union cause with a patriotism that was uncompromising"; who, when a local dancing school opened "under the tuition of a colored man," took his family there as a public gesture, to show that he did not find it contaminating to have a dark-skinned man teaching movement to his children.[23] Some of what we know of this man comes, moreover, from a family document that likely helped preserve his father's memory for young Stephen: a little biographical memoir written by Stephen's mother, whose final self-conscious sentence was possibly not lost on their son: "We laid his body away under the evergreens," she wrote at the close of her tribute, "amid the scenes of his childhood, as a flood of golden sunshine burst upon the scene."[24] Whether or not this is the source of Crane's coda for the Appleton edition of *The Red Badge,* his father was enormously more than a figure against whom Stephen merely reacted. Much more than a purveyor of stale religious sentiment, he was a committed participant in his country's sorest trial, and he furnished the best clue to Crane's initial concerns as a writer. It is worth emphasizing that for Stephen Crane, whose life was barely long enough for retrenchments or departures, the initial concerns were the enduring ones.

Like Hemingway, Crane began as a reporter, writing "sketches" of seaside New Jersey for his brother Towneley's Asbury Park News Bureau. Characteristically oblique, the early prose is worth reading not as journalistic hackwork but as a stylistic incarnation of his father's social criticism. Here, for example, is the elder Crane's tract on *Popular Amusements* (1869), a book that treats a range of recreations – theater, horse racing, dancing, novel reading, billiards, chess, and, in this case, baseball: "The publicity of the performance destroys all the good that might otherwise result from it, and, instead of play, makes it a mere exhibition, whose aim is not rest but notoriety." As this remark makes clear, it is worse than a convenience to describe the elder Crane as a man with a prudish scowl who recommended "total abstinence" from amusement. Capable of finer discrimination, he wrote a number of nondoctrinal books that have been treated as manifestations of the prohibitionist spirit against which his son supposedly rebelled, but that can be better understood as expressions of the old evangelical conviction that it matters not so much what one does as the spirit in which one does it. The baseball jeremiad swells in the hands of the elder Crane with indignation at the "very serious business" of Sunday sport, "involving as it does, the fortunes and the fame of the association in its future contests for championships and newspaper honors." One can readily imagine what the Reverend Crane would have thought, say, of the Washington Redskins' pregame prayer sessions: "Speeches, too, are made by the talking members of each club, expressive of the most intense admiration of each other's prowess, and breathing unutterable friendship."[25] The problem with American sport was nothing inherent in the game but was already, in 1869, its nature as a public exhibition – where the spectators' glee and rivalry were more significant than the exuberance of the players. It was in order to expose precisely this same social transition throughout American life that Jonathan Crane's son became a writer.

66

Because of the brevity and compactness of his life and writings, it is more seemly with Crane than with most major American writers to venture a comprehensive statement about his intentions: From the earliest sketches to *The O'Ruddy*, he was ultimately concerned with the moral deficiency of spectatorship. This is clear enough in "The Monster," a story about one black man's courageous intervention to save the life of a white child, an event that leaves the boy's father (who feels obliged to harbor the disfigured man) counting the unused teacups in his cupboard while his neighbors hold themselves aloof in racist disgust. It is equally clear in *The Red Badge*, especially in the moving scene in which Crane gives us the tattered man's panicked recognition that he is about to be deserted – a piece of writing flooded by compassion, entirely free of ironic distance, and openly angry at the uncommitted Fleming. In this act of desertion Henry seems almost reptilian as, with flushed brow, he "turned away suddenly and slid through the crowd." He worries his buttons like a finger-nervous child in need of relief; the whole spectacle is meant to be faintly disgusting.

The beginnings of Crane's anger at this kind of detached immaturity (an anger, I am suggesting, from which he does not spare himself) are detectable in muted, sardonic form even in the earliest sketches. There is, for example, a little piece produced in the summer of 1888 about "Avon's School by the Sea," one of those increasingly popular "schools at seaside and mountain resorts [where] people in their thirst for knowledge might combine the cool breezes . . . with useful instruction and entertainment." The portraits of promenading matrons and their sun-softened husbands are as derisive as anything in *The Red Badge*: "In Madame Alberti's classes in physical culture, it is interesting to note the look of surprise on people's faces, many of them showing the marks of age, when they learn for the first time the proper way to pick up articles from the floor or the scientific method of taking a chair" But the real force of the piece is lodged in its grammatical strategy – in its wickedly placed prepositions and participles: "The teachers and instructors are all of *recognized* ability. . . . The learned members of the institute are already *making their appearance* with their baggage at the hotels and boarding houses. . . . [The] genial manner [of Professor Conrad Diehl of New York] has already made him many friends here and his lectures are of *intense interest to* his enthusiastic pupils."[26] The tourist game of self-display, of "making their appearance," is Crane's first literary theme. He commits himself to no statements of value. He is not reporting intrinsic properties of character so much as the pantomime of social relations, which is little more than endless exhibitionism. Yet even here, just beneath the first level of tone, there can be felt the pressure of better social alternatives that are receding beyond his grasp. The feeling of the piece, though its meanings are nearly muted by their burial in syntax, is cumulative and unmistakable: Ability, as long as it is recognized, need not be real in this resort; the manufacture of "appearance" is the business of Asbury Park; the interest of Professor Diehl's lectures is not intrinsic, but resides in the approval of his audience. There is an embryonic theory of perception here, a rehearsal for *The Red Badge.*

For Crane – though he never developed an abstract vocabulary to identify this problem that was always embodied in his style – the meaning of human utterance became much more a function of the auditor's perception than of the speaker's intention. Communication becomes a version of the child's game of telephone: Intention is always getting lost in a chain of misperceptions. It is not hard to imagine him reading R. D. Laing's *The Politics of Experience* (1967) with an approving sense of *déjà vu:* "I cannot experience your experience. You cannot experience my experience. We are both invisible men. All men are invisible to one another."[27] (Ellison's admiration for Crane's fiction, one may suggest, is grounded in his recognition that it is populated by invisible men unconscious of their invisibility.) An 1894 piece, "An Experiment in Misery," for example, presents the mind as working through a process of metaphoric substitution triggered by visual stimuli; sometimes the initiating object is a person, sometimes a thing: "A saloon stood with a voracious air on a corner. A sign leaning against the front of the doorpost announced: 'Free hot soup tonight.' The swing doors snapping to and fro like ravenous lips, made gratified smacks as the saloon gorged itself with plump men, eating with astounding and endless appetite, smiling in some indescribable manner as the men came from all directions like sacrifices to a heathenish superstition." The mind here is a maker of similes, a process that Crane as narrator both exploits and distrusts: A door opens, and "unholy odors rushed out like released fiends." The young man of the sketch (who is feigning poverty to see what the flophouse world is like) stares at his fellow vagrants sprawled on their cots, "heaving and snoring with tremendous effort, like stabbed fish." Finally, he lies awake, "carving biographies for these men from his meager experience." Experience is an inadequate basis for understanding, but the mind cannot be restrained from its habitual processes, from projecting meaning onto the "black figures, changing, yet frieze-like" that parade past the interpreting eye. The fact is that the young man of "An Experiment in Misery" has not the slightest idea of the internal experience of his flophouse companions; he has only an animating imagination that makes a monster out of a saloon. He – once again, the self-critical Crane – is the same mental being as Fleming, whose "accumulated thought . . . was used to form scenes." The observer imposes similes, which in turn impose histories, on the raw material of perception – namely, other human beings.

Throughout his career, then, Crane seems to suspect that language itself is a system of metaphoric deception: "The dead man and the living man exchanged a long look," he writes early in *The Red Badge*, bringing characteristically into focus what may be termed the junction between visual experience and the will to believe, just as he had done with "the dead man forced a way for himself." There is, of course, no "exchange" here at all, no "fraternizing" with nature, as he calls it later in the novel, though the first impulse of the observing mind is to surmise just such a fraternal exchange. Crane encourages his reader, in Wolfgang Iser's phrase, to "oscillate . . . between the building and the breaking of illusions."[28] Like James, Crane was obsessed with the figure of the observer, who is frequently a version of himself, and in beguilingly conventional sentences he suggests again and again how difficult it is for anyone to speak, much less to think, in a language that respects the integrity of the objects it describes: to remember that dead men simply do not see. Before *The Red Badge*, Crane's narrators tend to occupy a middle distance between subject and object, commenting amusedly on the failures of mutual perception that characterize their relations. One imagines, for instance, the narrator of *Maggie* swinging his head like a spectator at a tennis game – toward Pete on one side, "his hair curled down over his forehead in an oiled bang . . . his patent leather shoes look[ing] like weapons"; toward Maggie on the other, who "perceived that here was the ideal man." The trouble with these phrases is that they are conceived not in sympathy but in condescension. Pressed into a dream life by poverty, Maggie revels in spectacle, but Crane grants her no Jamesian charm; she is not a prototype of the enchanting Daisy Miller, but of Edith Wharton's obtuse Charity Royall:

> Maggie [at the theater] lost herself in sympathy with the wanderers swooning in snow-storms beneath happy-hued church windows, while a choir within sang "Joy to the World." To Maggie and the rest of the audience this was transcendental realism. Joy always within, and they, like the actor, inevitably without. Viewing it, they hugged themselves in ecstatic pity of their imagined or real condition. (Chap. 8)

"The schoolboy and schoolgirl," Stephen's father had written with similar distaste, "the apprentice, the seamstress, the girl in the kitchen, can conjure up rosy dreams as readily as other people; and perhaps more readily, as it requires but little reading of the sort to render them impatient of their lot in life, and set them to imagine something that looks higher and better."[29] To the elder Crane, literature was improperly inciting for middle-class children whose lives would never touch glamor. For Stephen (who called the popular fiction of his day "pink valentines"), most writers encouraged a form of psychic entrapment. Both Cranes, I would suggest, understood their own writing as something different, as a form of homily, capable of breaking their audience free from the voyeuristic solipsism that they found widespread in American life. Jonathan Crane's chief means toward this end had been to make use of scripture; Stephen Crane's was to invent a homiletic style of his own:

> The lieutenant of the youth's company was shot in the hand. He began to swear so wondrously that a nervous laugh went along the regimental line. The officer's profanity sounded conventional. It

relieved the tightened senses of the new men. It was as if he had hit
his fingers with a tack-hammer at home.
   He held the wounded member carefully away from his side, so
that the blood would not drip upon his trousers. (*Red Badge*,
Chap. 4)

The last sentence in this passage contains the essence of Crane's
genius, for in *The Red Badge* he has moved beyond condescension
to sympathetic identification. What he has done here is to collapse,
with a single observed detail, the usually unbridgeable distance
between observer and observed. This is a sentence that forces us
into intimacy with the lieutenant's experience, with his bodily
pain and residual sense of dignity. It is tactile writing, writing from
which one English reviewer received "the feeling of being pelted
from different angles by hail – hail that is hot," a kind of writing
that has been called (by Perry Miller, who was remarking not on
fin-de-siècle impressionism but on eighteenth-century revivalism)
"the rhetoric of sensation": "To have an actual idea of any pleasure or delight, there must be excited a degree of that delight. So to
have an actual idea of any trouble or kind of pain, there must be
excited a degree of that pain or trouble." Crane wrote in pursuit of
this kind of actuality, and he deployed his tactile style knowing full
well that what needed to be eradicated (and replaced by sensation)
were the abstractions – war, retreat, victory, even wound – that
resided, without creating discomfort, in his readers' minds. It is
quite true that Crane's prose has a certain merciless intensity and
that its "quick changes and contrasts in perspective . . . only just
miss being disagreeably affected."[30] He was willing to try anything
– sometimes too much – in order to preserve experience from
being lost in the numb places of the mind.
   The Red Badge of Courage is thus a book that cannot be read for
long in a state of mental relaxation. From the start, it strikes almost
lulling notes in the reader's mind, only to force them out of harmony into dissonance:

The cold passed reluctantly from the earth and the retiring fogs
revealed an army stretched out on the hills, resting. As the landscape changed from brown to green the army awakened and began
to tremble with eagerness at the noise of rumors. It cast its eyes
upon the roads which were growing from long troughs of liquid

mud to proper thoroughfares. A river, amber-tinted in the shadow of its banks, purled at the army's feet and at night when the stream had become of a sorrowful blackness one could see, across, the red eye-like gleam of hostile camp-fires set in the low brows of distant hills.

Once, a certain tall soldier developed virtues and went resolutely to wash a shirt. He came flying back from a brook waving his garment, banner-like. He was swelled with a tale he had heard from a reliable friend who had heard it from a truthful cavalryman who had heard it from his trust-worthy brother, one of the orderlies at division head-quarters. He adopted the important air of a herald in red and gold. (*Red Badge,* Chap. 1)

The modulation from brown to green, indeed the orchestration throughout the passage of images of awakening, is a process by which Crane raises expectations in the reader's mind with the express purpose of deflating them: There is to be no collective awakening for this army; the oracular authority of the tall soldier – introduced early as the conventional messenger of tragic drama – is soon exposed as fraudulent. It is in this sense that *The Red Badge* is written in cooperation with the reader, who, Crane knows, brings to it a load of ideological and even literary assumptions.

What is happening in the opening paragraphs of *The Red Badge* is the identification and destruction of predispositions in the reader's mind, which is an experience exactly parallel to that which Henry Fleming undergoes. Fleming, like the cooperative reader, learns to shed at least some of his controlling assumptions about the meaning of what he sees, and is left in a new state of openness by the novel's end. It is that openness that makes it possible to read *The Red Badge* as a *Bildungsroman* and that helps to explain Crane's uncertain shifts between the manuscript and the Appleton edition as he searched for a balance between exposing Fleming's symbol-making imagination and celebrating his reeducation into a kind of epistemological purity. But whichever text we prefer, it is clear that Crane, in revising, was uncertain over the *extent*, not the desirability, of Fleming's commitment to real human fellowship. The closing pages present the world as a remarkable amalgam between a Darwinian crucible – "with his new eyes he could see that the secret and open blows which were being dealt about the world with such heavenly lavishness were in truth blessings" – and Christian communitarianism – "It was a deity laying about him with the bludgeon of correction." One of the corrigible victims of this deity is Henry Fleming, by whom the tattered man, "blind with weariness and pain, had been deserted in the field." What Crane yearned to achieve, for himself as well as for his character, was a state of mind freed from the isolating power of the solitary imagination. Toward this end, he was even willing to speak about God as the agent of deliverance. All the while he missed, and tried to retrieve, what he unashamedly called in one of his sketches "a memory of the old days" – which he increasingly associated with his pious fathers. (Near the end of his life he thanked one of them, a former teacher at Syracuse, for having once made the effort to pass on something of value to an unreceptive fraternity boy: "I can only hope that you will remember the lad who . . . often tells about his fireside the tale of the man who exhorted him . . . with . . . kindliness and interest – indeed almost affection.")[31] Crane was grateful for any tutelary kindness because it meant to him that there were still some who believed in unimpeded dialogue between one generation and the next, indeed between one man and the next. He was, in *The Red Badge,* trying to restore something of that dialogue, which is finally what makes the episodes with the tattered man so moving. As Crane tried, he learned more and more about his own estrangement from his nation's taxing past, and about how little most of his contemporaries concerned themselves with one another in the present. Only by grasping Crane's incipient historical awareness – undeveloped as it is, even furtive – can we fully understand the leading characteristic of his prose: the wistfulness beneath the iconoclasm. The Civil War was his subject because he sensed in it the final collapse of whatever American community there once had been – something that he could only barely imagine, but that flickers always as a faint possibility at the edge of his realism.

Perhaps the most acute comment on Crane's spiritual need is a remark by Joseph Conrad, who knew him in his last months at Brede:

> It was on the ground of the authorship of that book [*The Nigger of the Narcissus*] that Crane wanted to meet me. Nothing could have

73

been more flattering, than to discover that the author of "The Red Badge of Courage" appreciated my effort to present a group of men held together by a common loyalty and a common perplexity in a struggle not with human enemies but with hostile conditions testing their faithfulness to the conditions of their own calling.[32]

Conrad strikes all the right notes. Having a common faith and a dignified calling (Conrad surely intended the religious resonance of that word) seemed, to the son of the Reverend Jonathan Crane, the most elusive and most necessary of experiences. Since he knew that he was not alone in missing them, he produced a body of work that may be read not only as self-pitying but also as a cry for his country.

NOTES

1. Melville, *Battle-Pieces*, ed. Sidney Kaplan (Amherst: University of Massachusetts Press, 1972), p. 265; F. Scott Fitzgerald, *Tender Is the Night* (New York: Scribners, 1934), p. 57.

2. Seward, quoted in Kenneth M. Stampp, *The Imperiled Union: Essays on the Background of the Civil War* (New York: Oxford University Press, 1980), p. 191; Daniel Aaron, *The Unwritten War: American Writers and the Civil War* (New York: Oxford University Press, 1973), p. 343.

3. Edmund Wilson, *Patriotic Gore: Studies in the Literature of the American Civil War* (New York: Oxford University Press, 1969), chap. 15; Twain, "The Story of a Speech," in Justin Kaplan, ed., *Great Short Works of Mark Twain* (New York: Harper's, 1967), p. 136; DeForest, *Miss Ravenel's Conversion* (New York: Rinehart, 1955), p. 274. Buchanan, quoted in Stampp, *The Imperiled Union*, p. 221.

4. Aaron, *The Unwritten War*, p. 211; Review quoted in R. W. Stallman, *Stephen Crane: A Life* (New York: George Braziller, 1968), p. 181.

5. Richard M. Weathersford, *Stephen Crane: The Critical Heritage* (London: Routledge & Kegan Paul, 1973), p. 86.

6. Donald Pease, "Fear, Rage, and the Mistrials of Representation in *The Red Badge of Courage*," in Eric J. Sundquist, ed., *American Realism: New Essays* (Baltimore: Johns Hopkins University Press, 1982), pp. 155–75.

7. Crane, "In the Depths of a Coal Mine," in William M. Gibson, ed., *The Red Badge of Courage and Selected Prose and Poetry* (New York: Rinehart, 1968), p. 323.

8. J. C. Levenson, ed., *Stephen Crane: Prose and Poetry* (New York: Literary Classics of the United States, 1984), p. 1365.

9. John Berryman, "Stephen Crane: *The Red Badge of Courage*," in Thomas A. Gullason, ed., *Stephen Crane's Career: Perspectives and Evaluations* (New York: New York University Press, 1972), p. 361; Alfred Kazin, *On Native Grounds* (London: Jonathan Cape, 1943), p. 68; Aaron, *The Unwritten War*, p. 215; Hamlin Garland, *Crumbling Idols* (1894) (Cambridge, Mass.: Harvard University Press, 1960), p. 65.

10. Lewis P. Simpson, "Identifying Southern Colonial Literature: The Problem of Historical Perspective," paper delivered at the 1984 convention of the Modern Language Association.

11. Bernard Weisberger, "*The Red Badge of Courage*," in Charles Shapiro, ed., *Twelve Original Essays on Great American Novels* (Detroit: Wayne State University Press, 1958), pp. 123, 121.

12. Alfred Kazin, Introduction to *The Red Badge of Courage* (New York: Bantam Books, 1983), p. xii; Letter to Nellie Crouse (Jan. 26, 1896), in *Stephen Crane: Letters*, ed. R. W. Stallman and Lillian Gilkes (New York: New York University Press, 1960), p. 105.

13. "Plans for Story" (dictated to Cora Crane), manuscript, Columbia University Library.

14. Ralph Ellison, "Stephen Crane and the Mainstream of American Fiction," in *Shadow and Act* (New York: Vintage, 1972), p. 75; Kazin, Introduction, p. xi; Theodore Roosevelt to Crane (Aug. 18, 1896), in Stallman and Gilkes, eds., *Letters*, p. 128.

15. J. C. Levenson, Introduction to *The O'Ruddy* (Charlottesville: University of Virginia Press, 1971), p. xxiv; Crane, "Plans for Story."

16. Miller, *Incident at Vichy* (1964), in *The Portable Arthur Miller* (New York: Viking, 1971), p. 339; Crane, "Plans for Story."

17. J. T. Crane, *Popular Amusements* (New York: Carlton and Lanahan, 1869), p. 123.

18. J. C. Levenson, Introduction to "Stephen Crane," in *Major Writers of America*, ed. Perry Miller (New York: Harcourt, Brace, 1962), 2, 392; Levenson, in ibid., 2, 388; Katz, Review of Chester L. Wolford, *The Anger of Stephen Crane: Fiction and the Epic Tradition*, in *Studies in American Fiction* 12 (1984):239.

19. Hoffman, *The Poetry of Stephen Crane* (New York: Columbia University Press, 1956), p. 13.

20. Aaron, *The Unwritten War*, p. 217; Weathersford, *Stephen Crane*, p. 97.

21. Bellow, *The Adventures of Augie March* (1953) (New York: Avon, 1977), pp. 10–11.

22. Bleich, quoted in Walter Benn Michaels, "The Interpreter's Self: Peirce on the Cartesian 'Subject,'" in Jane P. Tompkins, ed., *Reader-Response Criticism: From Formalism to Post-Structuralism* (Baltimore: Johns Hopkins University Press, 1980), p. 199.

23. Mrs. Helen Crane, "Rev. Jonathan T. Crane, D. D.," in Gullason, ed., *Stephen Crane's Career*, pp. 14, 33, 19.

24. Ibid., p. 35.

25. J. T. Crane, *Popular Amusements*, pp. 84, 79, 82–83.

26. Levenson, ed., *Stephen Crane*, pp. 454–5 (italics added).

27. R. D. Laing, *The Politics of Experience* (New York: Ballantine, 1967), p. 18.

28. Wolfgang Iser, "The Reading Process: A Phenomenological Approach," in Tompkins, ed., *Reader-Response Criticism*, p. 62.

29. J. T. Crane, *Popular Amusements*, pp. 136–7.

30. Weathersford, *Stephen Crane*, p. 97; Miller, "The Rhetoric of Sensation," in *Errand into the Wilderness* (Cambridge, Mass.: Harvard University Press, 1956), p. 178; Warner Berthoff, *The Ferment of Realism* (New York: Cambridge University Press, 1981), p. 228.

31. Crane to the Rev. Charles J. Little in Stallman and Gilkes, ed., *Letters*, pp. 208–9.

32. Conrad, quoted in Nicholas Delbanco, *Group Portrait: A Biographical Study of Writers in Community* (New York: William Morrow, 1982), pp. 59–60.

4

The Spectacle of War in Crane's Revision of History

AMY KAPLAN

1

THE year that saw the publication of *The Red Badge of Courage* to great acclaim on both sides of the Atlantic was reviewed as a time of "wars and bloodshed" by Joseph Pulitzer's New York *World*. The newspaper's year-end survey of 1895 recalled that "from Japan westward to Jackson's Hole, bloodshed has encircled the globe," and it listed some examples of contemporary wars:

> When the year 1895 dawned the Italians were engaged in a bloody war with the Abyssinians; Haiti was overrun by rebels, who had burned the capital, Port-au-Prince, and slaughtered many people; the French were preparing for their disastrous if victorious war in Madagascar; the Dutch were slaughtering the natives of Lombok, one of their dependencies in southeastern Asia; and rebellions were in progress in several of the South American countries.[1]

To newspaper readers in 1895, these outbreaks of international violence may have seemed remote from America's geographical borders and even more distant in time from the historic battlefields of America's last major conflict, the Civil War. Yet as the decade progressed, the United States ventured more boldly into international disputes; after verging on military engagements with Italy, Chile, and Britain in the early 1890's, America fought a war against Spain in Cuba and the Philippines in 1898. Mass-circulation newspapers like the *World*, which had already made exotic battles in European colonies a staple for American consumption, had an enthusiastic audience feasting on the spectacle of the Spanish-American War. One year after covering the Greco-Turkish War, Stephen Crane landed in Cuba with the American marines as a special correspondent for Pulitzer. Datelined June 22, 1898, the

77

World headline for the first major battle of the Spanish-American War read: "THE RED BADGE OF COURAGE WAS HIS WIG-WAG FLAG."[2]

What do these international wars have to do with *The Red Badge of Courage*, a novel begun in 1893 about an internecine conflict that took place thirty years earlier? Although Crane himself had not yet seen a battle when he wrote his book, the heightened militarism in America and Europe at the end of the nineteenth century shapes his novel as much as does the historical memory of the Civil War. Crane's novel participates in a widespread cultural movement to reinterpret the war as the birth of a united nation assuming global power and to revalue the legitimacy of military activity in general. The novel looks back at the Civil War to map a new arena into which modern forms of warfare can be imaginatively projected.

This conjunction of past and present may help explain the paradoxical status that *The Red Badge of Courage* has long held as *the* classic American Civil War novel that says very little about that war. Crane divorces the Civil War from its historical context by conspicuously avoiding the political, military, and geographical coordinates of the 1860s, and he equally divorces the conflict from a traditional literary context by rejecting generic narrative conventions. The novel reduces both history and the historical novel to what its main character thinks of as "crimson blotches on the page of the past." The illegibility of history in Crane's war novel has informed most critical approaches, which either treat it as a statement about war in general, turn war into a metaphor for psychological or metaphysical conflicts, reconstruct the absent historical referents of the Civil War battlefield, or decry the weakness of the historical imagination in American literature. Contrary to these critical assumptions, Crane wrenches the war from its earlier contexts, not to banish history from his "Episode" but to reinterpret the war through the cultural lenses and political concerns of the late nineteenth century.

If, on the battlefield of *The Red Badge of Courage*, Crane does not revisit old territory with a historical imagination, he does explore an unfamiliar social landscape reminiscent of the modern cityscape of his earlier writing and replete with similar social tensions. Like other well-known novels of its time, Crane's is a book about social change, about the transition not only from internecine to international conflict or from preindustrial to mechanized forms of warfare, but also from traditional to modern modes of representation. The novel implicitly contributes to and criticizes the contemporary militarization of American culture by focusing not on politics but on the problem of representing war. Crane transforms the representation of war from a shared experience that can be narrated in written or oral stories into an exotic spectacle that must be viewed by a spectator and conveyed to an audience. This transformation was to provide Crane with a lens for reporting the real wars he observed in Greece and Cuba only two years after writing his Civil War novel.

2

To read *The Red Badge of Courage* historically, it is necessary to understand how Crane's contemporaries were reinterpreting the Civil War, for Crane was not alone in divorcing the conflict from its historical context and formulating a new one. In the outpour of nonfiction and fiction in the 1880s, writers consistently avoided referring to political conflicts over slavery or secession in favor of the theme of national reconciliation.[3] In both genteel magazines and dime novels, the "road to reunion" took the form of glorifying the heroism and valor of the soldiers in both armies. Memoirs of the war depicted soldiers on both sides chatting and singing together on guard duty and cheering one another in the midst of battle as they rescued the wounded. Such memories led one author to conclude that "had the work of reconstruction been left to the fighting men of the North and South, much of the bitterness of that period would have been avoided."[4] The bonds between soldiers in the field were seen to outlast and transcend the political conflicts for which they fought.

Crane's source for *The Red Badge of Courage*, the popular *Battles and Leaders of the Civil War*, epitomized this trend. To instruct a new generation in the meaning of the war in 1884, the editors of *The Century Magazine* invited veterans from both the Union and Confederate armies to record in detail their memories of major battles with the purpose of facilitating mutual respect, "the strongest bond of a united people.''[5] In their preface to the four-volume edition in 1887, the editors took partial credit for that fact that

> coincident with the progress of the series during the past three years may be noted a marked increase in the number of fraternal meetings between Union and Confederate veterans, enforcing the conviction that the nation is restored in spirit as in fact, and that each side is contributing its share to the new heritage of manhood and peace.[6]

These memoirs and meetings radically reinterpreted the meaning of the battlefield itself. No longer an arena for enacting political conflict, it became a site for transcending conflict through the mutual admiration of military prowess.

Fiction about the Civil War in the 1880s reinforced the theme of reconciliation by using romantic subplots to frame the battle scenes. In the traditional genre of the historical romance, heroism on the battlefield was rewarded by the love of the heroine at home; the plots often revolved around a love affair between a Union soldier and a Southern girl or around the division and reunion of kinsmen fighting on opposing sides. If memoirs hailed the reunion among men on the battlefield, fiction suggested that ''neither the war nor reconstruction produced problems which could not be solved . . . by an adequately consummated marriage.''[7] During the postreconstruction period, both military histories and domestic fiction excised political conflict from the collective memory of the Civil War.

If the spirit of national unity could be abstracted from the devastating four-year conflict, the ideal of martial valor could be further abstracted from the goal of national unity. Participants and observers alike later viewed the battlefield of the Civil War as a testing ground for the virility and courage of the individual soldier, independent of any broader national aim. Oliver Wendell Holmes, Jr., for example, in his famous *Memorial Day Address* of 1895, lauded martial heroism as a value in itself, rather than as a means to a political or moral end. In the same year as the publication of *The Red Badge of Courage*, he stated:

> I do not know the meaning of the universe. But in the midst of doubt, in the collapse of creeds, there is one thing that I do not doubt . . . and that is that the faith is true and adorable which leads

a soldier to throw away his life in obediance to a blindly accepted duty, in a cause which he little understands, in a plan of campaign of which he has no notion, under tactics of which he does not see the use.[8]

By the 1890s, Holmes could wrench the battlefield from the social and historical context of the war in which he himself had fought, and could transform it into a figurative crucible for the test of individual manhood – a figuration that Crane's revisions put to the test.

Holmes reinterpreted the Civil War as a model for an emerging ethos that Theodore Roosevelt soon dubbed "the strenuous life." Whereas Holmes glorified the chastening discipline of the battlefield, others sought to revive those aristocratic and chivalric values repressed by the routinization of industrial life. The revival of the martial ideal, according to historian John Higham, was part of the broader "reorientation of American culture in the 1890s" toward the celebration of youth, combativeness, and muscularity.[9] This shift redefined masculinity in terms of aggressive and physical activism – now opposed to effeminacy – to supplant the older Victorian emphasis on self-discipline and responsibility – opposed primarily to childhood. Such a reorientation found a wide range of expressions, from the craze for outdoor activities and the movement to conserve the wilderness, to the intellectual recognition of the formative qualities of the frontier, to the popular enthusiasm for competitive athletics and spectator sports. A common denominator of these different cultural forms was the discovery of "the primitive" as a regenerative force against what some called the enervation of "overcivilization." "A saving touch of old fashioned barbarism," in the words of a sports enthusiast, could be found equally in the untamed wilderness, in the athletic arena, or on the battlefield.[10] Touching on all three realms, Crane reportedly confessed to Hamlin Garland that "his knowledge of battle had been gained on the football field, 'The psychology is the same. The opposite team is an enemy tribe!'"[11] Crane's vocabulary locates his Civil War battlefield at the intersection of militarism, athleticism, and primitivism in the 1890s.

In fiction, the discovery of the primitive and the celebration of the martial ideal joined together in trends as diverse as naturalism

81

and the historical romance. The adventure tales of Robert Louis Stevenson were more widely read in the United States than in England, and Kipling remained one of the most popular writers in both countries throughout the 1890s. Kipling's *The Light that Failed* (1891), with its double focus on the bohemian artist in Europe and the imperial battlefields of the Orient, exerted a strong influence on American naturalists such as Crane, Norris, and London. While they explored the atavistic qualities of modern life and often universalized war as a metaphor for the social Darwinian struggle, the historical romance, which appealed to a similar ethos, underwent a popular revival on both sides of the Atlantic.[12] Sir Walter Scott's novels were reprinted and acclaimed not for their historicity but for their depiction of vigorous and virile action, and they were joined by new chivalric romances such as Robert Louis Stevenson's *Prince Otto* (1885), F. Marion Crawford's *Saracinesca* (1887), Anthony Hope's *Prisoner of Zenda* (1894), Richard Harding Davis's *The Princess Aline* (1895), and Charles Major's *When Knighthood Was in Flower* (1898).[13] Whether set in historical or mythical kingdoms, these novels stressed neither courtly behavior nor political intrigue, but the freewheeling and lawless spirit of the medieval knight, who best demonstrated his skill and valor through acts of raw physical violence.

In the 1890s, the figure of the medieval warrior combined primitive virility with an appeal to the contemporary concern for the purity of the Anglo-Saxon race. As Frank Norris claimed in his first novel, "somewhere deep down in the heart of every Anglo-Saxon lies the predatory instinct of his Viking ancestors – an instinct that a thousand years of respectability and tax-paying have not quite succeeded in eliminating."[14] According to historian Jackson Lears, the attraction to the medieval knight expressed a yearning for "real life," for a personal wholeness that could rejuvenate an insecure elite who felt threatened both by the "weightlessness" of their own lives and by the unruliness of the classes beneath them. Whereas the feudal lord appealed to readers with the iron fist he wielded over his vassals, bloody battles between knights in exotic lands compensated for the ennui resulting from the subordination of primal instincts to commercial needs.[15] In addition, reading about battles fought single-handedly with swords and brute strength fulfilled a longing for warfare untainted by the mechanization initiated in the Civil War and intensified during the half-century that followed.

Nevertheless, romances about crusaders, questing knights, and fantastic kingdoms did not only look back nostalgically toward a lost wholeness; they also projected fanciful realms for contemporary adventures and the exercise of military power. William Dean Howells was not the only critic to relate the "swashbuckler swashing on his buckler" to the arousal of jingoism and the clamor for foreign wars in the 1890s.[16] The lament for the closing of the frontier was often coupled with a call for opening new frontiers abroad to release the pressure of class conflict brewing at home, and the discovery of the primitive – in the wilds and within – similarly coincided with the discovery of primitive people to control in exotic places. Chivalric nostalgia existed side by side with the rationalization and modernization of the armed forces; the critique of overcivilization bolstered the onward march of "civilization," and the discovery of barbaric impulses within modern man would be enacted on a battlefield of "uncivilized" frontiers, such as Cuba and the Philippines.[17]

In his speech delivered in 1899, "The Strenuous Life," Theodore Roosevelt clearly summarized these connections between the Civil War, the martial ideal, and empire building. Opening with a reference to Lincoln and Grant, Roosevelt used the war as evidence of the "iron in the blood of our fathers" and called on his own generation to follow their example by embodying "those virile qualities necessary to win in the stern strife of actual life." The Civil War, he argued, placed "the mighty American republic once more as a helmeted queen among nations." His specific motive was to convince his audience to accept "the white man's burden" by annexing the Philippines, which had been recently occupied in the Spanish-American War. American "conduct toward the tropic islands," he claimed, was "merely the form which our duty has taken at the moment" to continue "the life of strenuous endeavor."[18] Roosevelt himself had just recently engaged in such a strenuous activity in the war with Spain by organizing and leading the volunteer regiment the Rough Riders, a collection of frontiersmen, displaced aristocrats, and Ivy League athletes. Stephen Crane, in his capacity as foreign correspondent, accompanied them on their well-publicized Cuban exploits, one of which he labeled a "gallant blunder."[19]

It is fitting that one of the best-sellers during the Spanish-American War was a novel about the Civil War, *The Song of the Rappahannock*, a book that rewrites *The Red Badge of Courage* by explicitly claiming that recruits did not act like Crane's hero. This novel, by Seymour Dodd, recapitulates those revisions of the Civil War we have traced through the 1880s and 1890s, which present not a "civil war" at all but a war that expunges internal conflicts. Dodd's preface reminds his readers that "memories of that older crisis can no longer be dividing or exclusive possessions, but each fragment of its story becomes part of the common heritage of American manhood." The second edition of the novel, published immediately after the Spanish-American War, spells out the fulfillment of this "heritage":

> on the heights of Santiago we see men of the South standing shoulder to shoulder with men of the North, mingling their blood victoriously under the old Flag, while the world looks on with admiration not unmixed with fear.[20]

Dodd's novel completes a circle of revisions that starts with the deletion of conflict from the Civil War battlefield by celebrating the martial valor of soldiers on both sides and ends with the fulfillment of the war's legacy by externalizing conflict as United States troops face foreign enemies abroad.

3

In *The Red Badge of Courage*, Crane not only contributes to the contemporary abstraction of the Civil War from its historical context but also takes the further step of challenging those popular tales that recontextualize the war. As Eric Solomon has established, parody provides a central narrative strategy in all of Crane's writing.[21] His war novel does more than parody either generic conventions or historical novels about the Civil War; it specifically parodies those narrative forms used to reinterpret the Civil War and to imagine new kinds of warfare in the 1890s.

The problem of reinterpreting the past to anticipate the immediate future is thematized in the first chapter of *The Red Badge of*

Courage. Following the silent panorama of the battlefield in the opening paragraph, the novel bursts into a noisy state of anticipation: To plot in advance their upcoming initiation, recruits trade rumors about "brilliant campaigns" and veterans exchange tales of former battles to reimagine the enemy they will soon face. The central character, Henry Fleming, reexamines the stories he has heard about war in order to question what course his own actions might take. Throughout the first chapter, the narrator similarly evokes contemporary narratives of the Civil War and of the chivalric romance to test their applicability to his own story that lies ahead.

The second paragraph of the novel mocks the revival of the medieval romance by using chivalric rhetoric to describe the mundane activity of a soldier doing his laundry: "Once a certain tall soldier developed virtues and went resolutely to wash a shirt. He came flying back from a brook waving his garment, banner-like. He was swelled with a tale." The pose the soldier adopts of "herald in red and gold" is similarly deflated by his news, which sounds like small-town gossip, "heard from a reliable friend who had it from a truthful cavalryman who had heard it from his trustworthy brother." Both the medium and the message of these insubstantial rumors reveal the powerlessness of the recruits and the inadequacy of their tales to anticipate their fate.

The third paragraph of the novel suggests the social function of these chivalric stories for readers at the end of the century. The rumors of "a brilliant campaign" draw an audience of soldiers away from "a negro teamster who had been dancing upon a cracker-box." In the 1880s, tales of chivalric exploits similarly superseded the older narrative of emancipation at a time when reconciliation was effected at the cost of undoing the gains of former slaves after the war. In this only reference to blacks in the novel, Crane both divorces his own "episode" from any former stories about freeing the slaves and calls attention to the process whereby the history of emancipation had been reduced to a form of entertainment. The "deserted" teamster sits "mournfully down" to lament his loss of an audience and his own passing as a figure for the subject of emancipation from the narrative landscape of the Civil War battlefield.

In the first chapter, Crane similarly evokes and discards the domestic subplot, which provided an important structure in both Civil War romances and regional fiction. Thwarting Henry's expectation of a noble farewell, his mother deflates his romantic aspirations and reminds him that he is "jest one little feller 'mongst a hull lot'a others." When the regiment leaves his village, Henry catches a glimpse of a "dark girl," whom he thinks grows "sad and demure at the sight of his blue and brass." Like the "negro teamster," the "dark girl" mourns her own passing from the novel as a figure of the domestic subplot. Throughout the novel, domestic images resurface only to deflate the martial ethos rather than to validate it, as troops are compared to women trying on bonnets or to brooms sweeping up the battlefield.

In addition to rejecting these narratives of emancipation and domesticity, Crane parodies the memoirs of veterans that were so popular in the 1880s. The first chapter presents a commonplace scene in which Henry recalls chatting with a Confederate sentinel:

> "Yank", the other had informed him, "yer a right dum good feller.' This sentiment, floating to him upon the still air, had made him temporarily regret war." (Chap. 1)

Here the familiar encomium for the valor of the enemy is reduced to barely articulate mutual recognition. Crane follows this set piece with the recruit's distrust of veterans:

> Various veterans had told him tales. Some talked of grey, be-whiskered hordes who were advancing, with relentless curses and chewing tobacco with unspeakable valor; tremendous bodies of fierce soldiery who were sweeping along like the Huns. Others spoke of tattered eternally-hungry men who fired despondent powder. (Chap. 1)

The veterans' accounts of the past prove no more reliable than the rumors that the recruits project about the future. These stories create a mythical alien enemy that no more prepares Henry for battle than the mirror image of the foe as a "dum good feller." Indeed, Henry finds that "he could not put a whole faith in veterans' tales, for recruits were their prey" (Chap. 1).

Crane's parody questions the pedagogical value of those memoirs that made up such popular works as *Battle and Leaders*. In a well-known letter, Crane dismissed these volumes for their content, for their lack of information about the subjective response to the battlefield – "they won't tell me what I want to know."[22] In the opening of his novel, he rejects them as a form, as a narrative mode inadequate not only for historical accuracy but also for the representation of warfare in the 1890s. More broadly, Crane undermines both the authority of veterans to transmit their knowledge to a younger generation of soldiers and the power of historical memory to assure continuity into the present.

Although the novel opens by dismissing equally the narrative of emancipation, the domestic subplot of fiction, and the memoirs of veterans, the chivalric narrative outlasts the others as the main character clings to it tenaciously. Like Emma Bovary or Lord Jim, Henry Fleming's inner aspirations are composed of ideas in the popular books he reads and clichés that circulate around him. Henry imagines himself most often as a medieval knight, who in his late-nineteenth-century manifestation combines violent adventure with primitive virility. If Henry's dreams are rendered as lurid chivalric exploits, his rational skepticism is also cast in the rhetoric of strenuosity. When Henry first considers enlisting, for example, he imagines battles to be "things of the bygone with his thought-images of heavy crowns and high castles" (Chap. 1). In Henry's suspicion of the present war, the narrator mocks the "warrior critique" of an overcivilized society by twice repeating the refrainlike formula: "Greeklike struggles would be no more. Men were better, or more timid. Secular and religious education had effaced the throat-grappling instinct or else firm finance held in check the passions." Like many of Crane's contemporaries, however, Henry hopes that the battle will prove him wrong and will thrust him beyond the mundane commercial world into a realm of primitive abandon.

Despite the narrative parody, Henry does find these hopes fulfilled on the battlefield, where he resurrects the image of the medieval warrior. As he anticipates the battle, for example, he imagines himself as a dragon fighter, and he later flees from "an onslaught of redoubtable dragons." When he does fight, after returning to the regiment, he sees himself as a medieval warrior who has finally penetrated the primitive depths:

It was revealed to him that he had been a barbarian, a beast. He had fought like a pagan who defends his religion. Regarding it, he saw that it was fine, wild and, in some ways, easy. He had been a tremendous figure, no doubt. By this struggle, he had overcome obstacles which he had admitted to be mountains. They had fallen like paper peaks and he was now what he called a hero. And he had not been aware of the process. He had slept and, awakening, found himself a knight. (Chap. 18/17)

After the next fight, he feels that he has reached a frontier and entered "some new and unknown land" (Chap. 20/19). Crane represents Henry's battle experience as the return to a premodern era, as the exploration of an uncivilized frontier, and as the recovery of a primitive self in a dreamlike preconscious state. Crane's language becomes enmeshed in the rhetoric of strenuosity that it parodies as his narrative discovers the primitive and revives the martial ideal on the Civil War battlefield of the 1890s.

4

Lacking the familiar signposts of historical and geographical names and dates, Crane's battlefield does indeed appear as a timeless new and unknown land, divorced from any particular social context. Yet Crane delineates a social dimension of his landscape, which both explains the appeal of the chivalric revival for the youth of the 1890s and circumscribes its limits. The social geography of *The Red Badge of Courage* resonates with the tensions of the late nineteenth century, a period in which warfare provided the most common vocabulary for the violent class conflicts that erupted in America's cities. From the Great Railroad Strike of 1877 to the Haymarket Riot of 1886 to the Pullman Strike of 1894, labor struggles pitted workers against local police and state militias and threatened to engulf the entire nation in an apocalyptic battle. Problems and solutions alike were articulated in martial language: In Edward Bellamy's popular novel of 1888, *Looking Backward,* the army provided the model for a peaceful industrial utopia, and in 1894 Coxey's "army" of the poor marched in protest on Washington. Some social critics, such as the missionary Josiah Strong, blamed the intensity of urban conflicts on the closing of the frontier and advocated United States expansion abroad, with its concomitant militarism, as the only relief for these domestic social conflicts.

Although it is a critical commonplace that Crane uses war as a metaphor for city life in his urban writing, it is less noted that he inverts this metaphor in *The Red Badge of Courage*. He describes the battlefield with urban metaphors that overlay the countryside and leave only traces of the rural landscape. The approaching army is described as a train, for example; soldiers become "mobs" and "crowds," and officers are compared to political bossess cajoling the masses.[23] The battle itself is repeatedly called a vast "machine" that produces corpses and works according to mysterious orders. The main character moves from a farm into an army whose conditions resemble those of the industrial city of the late nineteenth century.[24] There he finds not the chivalric adventures he sought but the anonymous and "monotonous life in a camp" (Chap. 1). He also finds a social structure that is ridden with class tensions between officers and privates. Indeed, the novel represents more verbal expressions of hostility and physical acts of violence between members of the Union army than against enemy troops, who remain invisible on the battlefield. We see an officer beating a frightened recruit, for example; a fellow soldier wounds Henry; and he engages in hand-to-hand combat only with the corpse of the Union color bearer who refuses to loosen his grip on the flag.

These social conditions of army life overwhelm Henry with a sense not simply of overcivilized ennui but, more importantly, of powerlessness. Outrage against his impotence provides his strongest motivation for acting, both when he runs away and when he fights, and it takes specific shape in his hatred of his superiors, a hatred that far outstrips any emotion directed toward the enemy. Henry's final feats of heroism are spurred by his resentment toward the conversation he overhears between two officers; expecting "some great, inner historical things," he and his friend instead listen to the officers refer to the troops as "mule-drivers." For Henry, this shockingly confirms his mother's prediction: "he was very insignificant. The officer spoke of the regiment as if he referred to a broom" (Chap. 19/18). The officers' conversation pierces Henry's chivalric sense of self with language that recalls those figures rejected by the narrator in the first chapter. Henry and his comrades replace the black teamster as the work horses of the industrial army, and their heroism is deflated by the domestic reference to brooms. Henry and his friend cannot directly express their "unspeakable indignation" at the officer, except by fighting even more viciously, to the point where they seem "like tortured savages" (Chap. 20/19).

Although Henry resents the machinery of war and the powerlessness it entails and envisions himself as a primitive warrior to escape from this machine, his atavistic fantasies, rather than offering him an escape, entrench him more solidly in the machinery of the army. In the midst of the fight, the officers he resents so vehemently become his comrades-in-arms, and they transcend internal friction in the heat of the battle. When the colonel praises the youth and his friend for their fervor, "they speedily forgot many things. The past held no error and disappointment. They were very happy and their hearts swelled with grateful affection for the colonel and the lieutenant" (Chap. 22/21). In 1894, a year of violent strikes in the midst of a major depression, the popular syndicated version of *The Red Badge of Courage* ended here, with the privates reconciled with their superiors. Although it would be simplistic to reduce the novel to a social allegory, the tensions between officers and privates, between social classes, are externalized and transcended on the battlefield, and the mob of soldiers is channeled into the machine. War is transformed from a means of expressing conflict to a way of purging internal social conflict, which was the argument set forth for overseas expansion in the 1890s.

In the longer version of the book published in 1895, Henry moves beyond this social reconciliation to the more abstract harmony between the individual and the machine: "he emerged from his struggles, with a large sympathy for the machinery of the universe." Once Henry has proven his manhood on the battlefield, the "gigantic machine" no longer serves as a metaphor for war. Instead, it becomes a symbol of a cosmic order that gently embraces the individual soldier. The martial ideal plays a mediating role in this reconciliation. Mechanical order and primitive abandon are interdependent discourses; Henry's stories of chivalric heroism both fuel and are swallowed up by the machinery of modern warfare. Thus, by fusing industrial and chivalric language, Crane exposes the function of the revival of the martial ideal and shows that it criticizes a rationalized and hierarchical social order only to reinforce it.

5

The transition Henry makes from his local rural home to a distended industrialized army parallels the cultural course taken to revise the Civil War in the late nineteenth century – from a local internecine conflict to a model for international warfare. In charting these movements, Crane's narrative enacts an analogous transition from traditional to modern modes of representation. In the description of Henry's first battle, the narrator presents an excess of similes, as though he were frantically searching for the appropriate one. One of these compares Henry to an artisan "at a task. He was like a carpenter who has made many boxes, making still another box, only there was a furious haste in his movements" (Chap. 5). As the battle proceeds, however, the rhythm of the carpenter cannot keep up with such a relentless pace, and the artisanal imagery cannot sustain the representation of mechanized warfare. When Henry runs away after a lull in the fighting and then returns to observe it, the narrative moves from the carpenter/soldier producing his own coffin to the "grinding of an immense and terrible machine" that produces corpses. Just as Henry abandons his artisanal framework before he can return to the industrialized army, the narrator must abandon traditional narrative modes to develop new strategies for representing modern warfare.

If the first chapter of *The Red Badge of Courage* undermines the popular stories that revise the Civil War in the 1890s, the novel proceeds to question the viability of storytelling itself, to reject it as an outmoded narrative form. One of Crane's most hostile reviewers, General McClurg of the *Dial*, attacked the novel not only for its lack of patriotism, as Donald Pease has shown, but also for the fact that it has "absolutely no story," which McClurg elaborates as the absence of a traditional plot with logical sequence and causality.[25] Along with other reviewers, the general expected a story line that both embedded the battle in a political framework and rooted Henry's actions in a cohesive narrative pattern. Crane's refusal to tell a story, however, extends beyond the denial of a traditional plot to challenge the oral and written tradition of story-telling – a mode of communication, as Walter Benjamin has shown, linked to an artisanal preindustrial culture and inadequate to the representation of modern warfare.[26]

The first part of the novel, before Henry rejoins the battle, is filled with references to aborted forms of storytelling. When Henry finds his self-knowledge undermined by army life, he reassures himself that "like as not this here story'll turn out jest like them others did" (Chap. 1). But neither Henry's story nor Crane's novel turn out "like them others": When Henry runs away, he deviates from the traditional plot of heroism and from the role of "a man of traditional courage" (Chap. 3). In response, Henry then tries to bridge this gap by telling new stories. When he first enters the forest, for example, he weaves a Darwinian tale around a squirrel that runs from a tossed pine cone, only to have that story immediately undermined by the staring corpse in the middle of the woods – "The dead man and the living man exchanged a long look" – which usurps any possible exchange of experience through speech. Henry's reassuring tale is replaced by the fear that "some strange voice would come from the dead throat and squawk after him in horrible menaces" (Chap. 7). This pattern is repeated throughout the first half of the book: As soon as Henry tries to tell a tale, make a speech, or ask questions, the sight of corpses – staring, laughing, or shrieking – silences him. Jim Conklin's death, for example, both arouses and mocks Henry's desire to deliver any angry "phillipic." In the face of Conklin's grinning corpse, Henry can barely articulate "hell – ," and then finds that "his tongue lay dead in the tomb of his mouth" (Chaps. 9, 10).

Stories in *The Red Badge of Courage* rarely communicate experience or forge solidarity among the soldiers; instead, they often appear as weapons and are described in martial metaphors such as "spears," "arrows," "missiles," and "shields." To defend himself against the attack he expects from his comrades Henry

> tried to be-think of him a fine tale which he could take back to his regiment and with it turn the expected shafts of derision. . . . He was much afraid that some arrow of scorn might lay him mentally low before he could raise his protecting tale. (Chap. 11).

Unable to control his tale, he imagines that his regiment will puncture his story by taunting him with his own name – "Where's Henry Fleming?" – thereby turning his name into "a slang phrase" (Chap. 11). By naming Henry in this manner for the first time in the novel, the narrator mocks the epic tradition that immortalizes the name of the hero by recounting his struggle with a foe. The youth's naming, in contrast, divorces the achievement of identity from the story of conflict and marks the failure of storytelling, which is reduced to the shorthand of the "slang phrase."

Soon after his naming, Henry receives his wound in response to another thwarted attempt to speak; the figurative attack of linguistic "arrows" and "shafts" turns into a literal attack with the butt of a rifle, which changes the course of the narrative. When Henry sees other men running with fright, he "had the impulse to make a rallying speech, to sing a battle-hymn but he could only get his tongue to call into the air: "Why – why – what – what's th' matter?" To find an answer, in the "centre of a tremendous quarrel," he grabs someone to speak to "face to face" (Chap. 13/12). But such direct communication proves impossible, because the youth can only stammer and the man can only respond by swinging his rifle. Henry's wound signifies the inefficacy of human speech on the battlefield. Although the air is filled with the noise of human voices, attempts to speak coherently are drowned out by the songs and "stentorian" speeches of guns, the prelinguistic shrieks of the fighting soldiers, the cursing of officers, and the laughter of corpses.

Crane further undercuts the power of storytelling through the figure of the "tattered man," who first appears among the wounded as a listener:

> There was a tattered man, fouled with dust, blood and powder stain from hair to shoes who trudged quietly at the youth's side. He was listening with eagerness and much humility to the lurid descriptions of a bearded sergeant. His lean features wore an expression of awe and admiration. He was like a listener in a country-store to wondrous tales told among the sugar-barrels. He eyed the storyteller with unspeakable wonder. His mouth was a-gape in yokel fashion. (Chap. 8)

This description caricatures the tattered man both as a country bumpkin and as a figure for the oral tradition of the tall tale. He

93

sees the battlefield as an extension of his rural community, in which identities are clearly delineated and nothing appears incongruous or out of context. Adapting every occurrence to the stories he expects to hear, he assumes, given the context, that Henry has a hidden wound; he cannot imagine instead that Henry has a hidden story, which would remove him from the context of the other wounded soldiers. When the tattered man grows delirious from his wounds, he confuses Henry with the friend and next-door neighbor who fought beside him on the battlefield. By renaming Henry "Tom Jamison," the tattered man attempts to absorb Henry into a rural storytelling tradition, seeing a wound that isn't there and a neighbor he doesn't know. When Henry abandons the tattered man wandering in the fields, the narrative abandons this figure for the listener who can both absorb and partake in the story.

In the dismissal of the tattered man and the transformation of stories into weapons, Crane removes his own representation of war from the oral tradition, from the realm of "experience which is passed on from mouth to mouth."[27] He replaces the tattered man with the man with the "cheery voice" who, thriving on incongruity, magically leads the youth back to the regiment. This figure is described through a curious amalgamation of images from fairy tales and urban fiction. With "the keenness of a detective and the valor of a gamin," he weaves his way through the mazes of the battlefield as though they were city streets (Chap. 13/12). In contrast to the tattered man, he makes no attempt to ask Henry questions, to listen to his stories, or to create any bond between them, even though he speaks incessantly. In fact, Henry never even sees his face.

Despite his brief appearance, this faceless guide plays a pivotal role in the narrative. A figure for the author, he allows the story to start again, to be retold as a tale of courage. Through this garrulous and faceless character Crane makes the major turning point in his narrative gratuitous and parodies storytelling by exposing its arbitrariness. Drawn to Henry by his wound, the guide understands it at face value, and Henry's regiment immediately recontextualizes it as a sign of his fighting. Crane thus underscores the divorce of storytelling from cumulative experience by making his own tale revolve around this empty sign.

6

If Crane rejects storytelling as inadequate to narrate the experience of modern warfare, what other mode of narration does he put in its place? Critics tend to treat Crane's parody as the shedding of illusions to achieve a more realistic representation, whether of detailed sensory perceptions or of internal subjective impressions. Yet *The Red Badge of Courage* does not undercut the conventions of the story to represent a more immediate reality; rather, it frames a new sense of the real as a highly mediated spectacle. If Crane decontextualizes war as a subject for the storyteller, he recontextualizes it as an object to be viewed by a spectator. His spectacles of warfare are contained in the act of seeing, without hinting at a broader framework or a deeper meaning, and they do not outlast the moment in which they are glimpsed. Crane's emphasis on seeing in *The Red Badge of Courage* does not bring the war closer to the reader; instead, it distances the reader as a spectator of improvised sketches and theatrical scenes.

The first paragraph of the novel, which surveys the panorama of the battlefield, ends by drawing our attention to the act of seeing: "when the stream had become of a sorrowful blackness one could see, across, the red eye-like gleam of hostile campfires set in the low brows of distant hills." This anonymous "one" introduces the disembodied eye, which, like the faceless soldier, guides us through the battlefield. As the scene darkens, the enemy comes into view like stage lights in a theater. Conflict is theatricalized when the viewer cannot escape being seen as well; we look out at the landscape only to find hostile eyes staring back, just as Henry sees corpses glaring at him. The first paragraph, then, introduces the visual mode of representation that frames and competes with those parodied stories that immediately follow.

In describing the battle, the narrator repeatedly highlights his own composition of the scene. The shooting of a soldier, for example, is presented as "the instant's spectacle of a man, almost over it, throwing up his hands to shield his eyes" (Chap. 20/19); the retreating cavalry appears as a "sketch in gray and red dissolved into a mob-like body of men" (Chap. 4); and a sleeping soldier is framed as "the picture of an exhausted soldier" (Chap. 14/13). In many such passages the nouns — for example, "spectacle" "picture," or "sketch" – dominate the sentence grammatically and draw attention away from the activity of fighting to the act of seeing. This focus has the effect of freezing all motion within a static snapshot-like frame. In contrast to a story, which weaves together events and actions in a continuous narrative, Crane's spectacles isolate discontinuous moments of vision.

Crane's visual effects should be contrasted to those spectacles that have long filled the historical novel, where they are integrated with storytelling. In Scott's novels, descriptions of martial processions, chivalric contests, and heraldic displays implicitly tell a tale; visual details delineate the contours of a social order, and colorful spectacles enact broader political or moral dramas. Crane's notorious use of color – the subject of many contemporary parodies – can be seen to parody the traditional descriptions of the historical romance. We read, for example, of "columns changed to purple streaks," of a "yellow light thrown upon the color of his ambition," of a "vast blue demonstration," of a "black procession of oaths," and of "the red sickness of battle." Although these colors tease us with their vividness, they have less a mimetic than a curiously opaque effect. They conspicuously deny any narrative beyond themselves and excise all vestiges of storytelling from visual description.

In contrast to Scott, Crane's use of color is antiemblematic; the "red badge" itself flaunts its overt symbolic qualities, while at the same time being divorced from any meaningful context. In *The Red Badge of Courage* even the flag – the ultimate political emblem – lacks any referential stability. When, at the end of the first battle, Henry sees the flags, he "felt the old thrill at the sight of the emblems" (Chap. 5). Yet the noise of more distant battles immediately throws this vision out of focus to make him aware that "the war is not directly under his nose." When he does look around, he is surprised by the discrepancy between the tranquil landscape and the chaotic battlefield, a gap that the flag cannot fill by centering his dispersed vision or by endowing the action with political significance. When Henry grabs the flag in a later battle, it lacks its own reference until he "endowed it with power," just as others must invest his wound with significance. In the absence of a narrative or political context, the meaning of emblems must be improvised in the momentary drama.

The color bearer provides an appropriate figure for the narrator, whose visual representations are less descriptive and emblematic than theatrical. While they freeze the action of the battle, they call attention to the bold strokes of the narrator, to his own power to sketch the scene with bravado. In the highly debated simile, for example, at the end of Chapter 9 – "the red sun was pasted in the sky like a fierce wafer" – the verb "pasted" draws attention to the theatricality of the narrator's gesture, as though the sun were used as a prop in a stage setting. This powerful yet elusive simile interrupts Henry's aborted attempt to speak heroically and usurps his undelivered phillipic with the narrator's own heroic gesture. In contrast to the youth's silence and immobility, the theatrical style of the narrator becomes the focus of the spectacle, and his composition of the scene provides the central heroic act.

Throughout the novel, the narrator places the reader in the position of a spectator by referring to the battlefield as a "stage" or a "tableau," and to the soldiers as actors, or by comparing them to football players. The characters themselves alternate between the roles of actor and spectator. When the recruits retreat during the first battle, for example, we read that they are "not even conscious of the presence of an audience" of veterans, and we watch an officer beat a recruit as the two are "acting a little isolated scene" (Chaps. 4, 5). When the fighting begins, we observe Henry watching the battle: "the youth forgetting his neat plan of getting killed, gazed spellbound. His eyes grew wide and busy with the action of the scene." His anticipation of the impending fight is compared to a child's anticipation of a circus parade (Chap. 5). When the battle stops, he immediately wants to "look behind him and off to the right and off to the left. He experienced the joy of a man who at last finds leisure in which to look about him" (Chap. 5). His pleasure stems not just from surviving the battle or fighting well but from surveying the scene, an act that provides a sense of control that storytelling lacks.

Immediately after Henry runs "like a blind man," he returns to the battlefield to see what he might be missing: "It is better to view the appalling than to be merely within hearing. The noises of the battle were like stones; he believed himself liable to be crushed" (Chap. 6). Not seeing is more threatening to his identity than not fighting. After retreating into the woods, he finds himself driven back to the battle to observe "the immense and terrible machine," for "its complexities and powers, its grim processes, fascinated him. He must go close and see it produce corpses" (Chap. 8). He does then witness such a production in the highly theatrical spectacle of Jim Conklin's death. Despite the horror of the scene, "he had a great desire to see, and to get news. He wished to know who was winning," as though he could contain the battle in the confines of a football game (Chap. 11). Henry's obsession with seeing suggests that he runs away, in part, to trade the role of actor for spectator, to gain both a sense of control and a vicarious thrill from observing the battle at a safe enough distance not to be crushed by it.

When Henry rejoins the fighting, he is described as a performer so absorbed in his role as to forget when the scene closes. While he continues to fire during the lull in the battle, his comrades become "spectators" watching him (Chap. 18/17). Only by fighting in an isolated scene separated from the context of a surrounding battle can Henry secure a reputation for himself among his fellow soldiers, who "now looked on him as a war devil." Henry does not achieve this identity through confrontation with the enemy – who has stopped firing – but by acting in an improvised one-man show before the audience of his regiment. Their awe-struck glances replace the staring corpses and reverse his earlier fear of his name becoming a slang phrase.

Henry's desire for vengeance against the officer who called him a mule driver is similarly expressed in theatrical terms. To retaliate against the man who had "dubbed him wrongly" he cannot imagine speaking back – or even fighting back – but he can envision his revenge in the picture of his own dead body: "his corpse would be for those eyes a great and salt reproach" (Chap. 23/22). This vision has more power for Henry than the thought of proving himself through his action or using speech to rename himself.

When Henry reenters the fray, he does not give up his desire to see. While holding the flag he has just taken in battle, he stops to survey the panorama of the battlefield:

> The youth, still a bearer of colors, did not feel his idleness. He was deeply absorbed as a spectator. The crash and swing of the great drama made him lean forward, intent-eyed, and his face working in

small contortions. Sometimes, he prattled, words coming unconsciously from him in grotesque exclamations. He did not know that
he breathed; that the flag hung silently over him, so absorbed was
he. (Chap. 23/22)

His absorption in the act of seeing makes communicative speech
both impossible and unnecessary. By grabbing the flag, he has
earned not only proof of his fighting prowess but also the right to
see, so that, as color bearer, he plays the role of both spectator and
actor. He gains the leisure to stand still and observe the fighting
around him at the same time that he serves as the focal point for
the rest of the troops. He can, for the first time, safely see and be
seen.

Memory in *The Red Badge of Courage* is also theatricalized. Henry
reviews his battle experiences as though he were observing an
array of pictures rather than narrating a sequence of events. After
the first battle, for example, we watch him "standing as if apart
from himself" while "he viewed the last scene" (Chap. 4). After
another battle, he finds "considerable joy in musing upon his
performances during the charge. . . . He recalled bits of color that
in the flurry had stamped themselves unawares upon his engaged
sense" (Chap. 23/22). The recollection of these "bits of color"
protects him from hearing "the bitter justice in the speeches of the
gaunt and bronzed veterans" who call up tales of less sanguine
memories.

In Henry's final assessment of his experience, he continues to
consider his acts "in spectator fashion." Henry's "procession of
memory" is described as though

> his public deeds were paraded in great and shining prominence.
> Those performances which had been witnessed by his fellows
> marched now in wide purple and gold, hiding various deflections.
> They went gaily with music. It was pleasure to watch these things.
> He spent delightful minutes viewing the gilded images of memory.
> (Chap. 25/24)

This spectacle of heroism is interrupted, however, by "the dogging
memory of the tattered soldier." His memory evokes a narrative of
events that disrupts the colorful procession. Yet Henry succeeds in
translating this story of the past into the language of spectatorship:

he saw his vivid error and he was afraid that it would stand before him all of his life. He took no share in the chatter of his comrades, nor did he look at them or know them save when he felt sudden suspicion that they were seeing his thoughts and scrutinizing each detail of the scene with the tattered soldier. (Chap. 25/24)

Once Henry contains the tattered man in the frame of a theatrical scene and cuts him off from a memory that can be recounted in a story, he can "put the sin at a distance" and find "in it quaint uses."

The theatrical quality of Crane's battlefield has important implications for the definition of manhood in *The Red Badge of Courage*. Critics have long debated whether or not Henry becomes a man by proving himself on the battlefield and whether he achieves a deeper self-knowledge. We can place this question in the context of the 1890s if we recall that to Crane's contemporaries, such as Holmes and Roosevelt, the battlefield provided an arena for recovering the whole self in acts of primitive virility, shorn of the veneer of bourgeois life. Crane shows, on the contrary, that the self realized through the spectacle of the battle is highly theatrical, and thus inherently tentative and unstable. Although *The Red Badge of Courage* is about the growth of a youth, it does not tell the story of a self that evolves from cumulative experience; rather, it displays a self that must be repeatedly improvised before the observer. In the novel, manhood does not emerge in the medium of conflict, from the classical struggle with a foe; instead it takes shape in the medium of the spectacle, from the relationship to a spectator. For Henry to become a man or to have a self, he needs to imagine an audience watching him, and can only represent his actions in the eyes of others, whether in the glances of his fellow soldiers, in the praises from the colonel, or in the fantasy of his own corpse viewed by the officer. This need for an audience helps explain why, when he runs away, he imagines himself being seen and laughed at by corpses; their stares preserve Henry's identity and keep him from his often expressed fear of being "swallowed up," a fate that for him is worse than death. Thus Crane's representation of war as a spectacle both adopts and subverts the interpretation of the battlefield as a crucible for virility, as well as the concept of manhood as an internal primal quality. The constant need for an audience on the battlefield both destabilizes and resocializes the identity of the "real man."

Martial valor has traditionally depended on the display of the soldier before an audience, whether through military parades, or chivalric contests, or in the written heroic record. In *The Red Badge of Courage* Crane undermines these traditional forms of spectatorship with his repeated references to the newspaper as the modern lens for composing and viewing the spectacle of war. When Henry runs away from the battle, he wonders about the form that the representation of his actions might take, and realizes that

> individuals must have supposed that they were cutting the letters of their names deep into everlasting tablets of brass or enshrining their reputations forever in the hearts of their countrymen, while, as to fact, the affair would appear in printed reports under a meek and immaterial title. (Chap. 8)

Immediately after reflecting about the ephemeral nature of the newspaper report, he comes upon an isolated field strewn with corpses that seems to provide evidence of this idea:

> On the far side, the ground was littered with clothes and guns. A newspaper, folded up, lay in the dirt. A dead soldier was stretched with his face hidden in his arm. (Chap. 8)

The description draws our vision to the newspaper before we notice the corpse. This narrative placement of the newspaper suggests its mediatory function in modern warfare, a role initiated during the Civil War – one of the first major wars to be reported on a mass scale – and intensified during the international wars of the late nineteenth century. Indeed, the newspaper becomes the disembodied eye that confers an identity on the fighting men and produces a spectacle for readers far away from the front. The placement of the newspaper in the landscape suggests that soldiers too rely upon the paper to read about themselves on the battlefield, and they thereby become both performers in and spectators of the same drama. Yet the appearance of the newspaper in this field of corpses also underscores its incongruity, as it lies on the ground cut off both from a living audience and from a meaningful context.

101

Crane's revision of the history and story of the Civil War as a spectacle links his imaginative rendition of a war he never experienced to his later career as a foreign correspondent, covering the the Greco-Turkish and Spanish-American wars in the late 1890s. Crane reportedly jumped at the chance to see a real war in order to prove that *The Red Badge of Courage* was "all right."[28] Although he may have found that these wars verified his realism, his reports and fiction also show that the framework of the spectacle established in the novel provided a lens peculiarly suited to view international warfare in the 1890s.

"Jingoism is merely the lust of the spectator," wrote a British contemporary of Crane's, J. A. Hobson, in one of the first major studies of imperialism. Hobson compared the vicarious aggression of a spectator at a sporting event to the emotions of the jingoist, who remains "unpurged by any personal effort, risk or sacrifice, gloating over perils, pains and slaughter of fellow men who he does not know, but whose destruction he desires in a blind and artificially stimulated passion of hatred and revenge."[29] "The lust of the spectator" is both gratified and further aroused only in the act of watching, which distances the viewer while tantalizing him with the possibility of action. According to Hobson, who served as a journalist in the Boer War, the newspaper plays a crucial domestic role in arousing the spectatorial lust that supports imperial ventures in remote territories. Coinciding with the development of a mass circulation press in Britain and the United States, the international conflicts of the late nineteenth century created a new need for foreign correspondents to bring home the meaning of wars that "did not directly concern the future of the two countries where the major reading-public resided."[30]

In America in the 1890s, the so-called yellow press of Hearst and Pulitzer was notorious not only for sensationalistic coverage of the Cuban rebellion and the subsequent Spanish-American War, but also for staging many of the spectacles they reported. When in 1896 the illustrator Fredric Remington complained to Hearst from Havana that nothing was happening, Hearst reportedly responded, "You furnish the pictures and I'll furnish the war."[31] To keep his promise, Hearst filled his front page with pictures of Spanish atrocities at the same time that he started the modern sports page.[32] Both Hearst and Pulitzer made the news they reported by sending reporters on special spy missions, by leading rescue campaigns of Cuban ladies, or by using their own yachts – carrying their reporters – to capture Spanish refugees.

These spectacles often featured the reporter himself as their chief actor. During the international wars between the Civil War and World War I, the foreign correspondent came into being as a professional writer with a public persona. Bylines changed from "from our own correspondent" to the attribution of personal names, and headlines sometimes included the name of the reporter, as in the case of a celebrity like Crane: "STEPHEN CRANE AT THE FRONT FOR THE WORLD," "STEPHEN CRANE'S VIVID STORY OF THE BATTLE OF SAN JUAN," and "STEPHEN CRANE SKETCHES THE COMMON SOLDIER."[33] Reporters often made themselves or their colleagues the heroes of their stories and the act of reporting the main plot. This focus turned writing into a strenuous activity and the reporter into a virile figure who rivaled the soldiers. If the private, Henry Fleming, tries to become a spectator of the same battle he fights, reporters, the professional spectators, often tried to become actors by engaging in combat. Crane himself both played and parodied the figure of the heroic correspondent by flaunting his indifference to bullets under fire and by capturing a Puerto Rican town in a mock invasion. The theatrical style of *The Red Badge of Courage* anticipates the aggrandizement of the act of reporting to overshadow the action on the battlefield.

By dramatizing the exploits of the reporter, newspapers transformed political and military conflicts in foreign colonies into romantic adventures in exotic landscapes. In addition, Crane suggests in his novel *Active Service* – based on his experience in the Greco-Turkish War – that the reporter also provided an important spectatorial function for the soldiers on the field, who

> when they go away to the fighting ground, out of the sight, out of the hearing of the world known to them and are eager to perform feats of war in this new place they feel an absolute longing for a spectator. . . . The war correspondent arises, then, to become a sort of cheap telescope for the people at home; further still, there have

been fights where the eyes of a solitary man were the eyes of the world; one spectator whose business it was to transfer, according to his ability, his visual impressions to other minds.[34]

This "cheap telescope" proved especially important on the battlefield of colonial territories, where enemy combatants often were both physically and ideologically invisible. Reports from Cuba commented on the difficulty American troops had in seeing the Spanish fighters, who sniped at them through the thick brush. After Spain surrendered, America's former allies, the Cubans and even more so the Filipinos, turned their guerrilla warfare against the Americans now occupying their lands. Whereas the European Spaniards were represented as equal, if hated, foes, the Cuban and Filipino guerrillas, even as allies, were represented not as soldiers fighting a real war but as criminal elements to subdue.[35] In the face of such invisible and shifting allies and enemies, the political context of the war often blurred. The reporter redrew the contours of a foreign terrain by dramatizing American action and identity in the eyes of the audience at home rather than in relation to a shadowy and less than human enemy. The promise of being seen through the medium of the newspaper compensates for the confusion and the fear of not seeing.

In *The Red Badge of Courage*, Crane had already developed the mechanisms of this cheap telescope by rendering the enemy invisible on the battlefield of the Civil War and by making the soldier's identity more contingent on an audience than on conflict with the foe. Many of Crane's newspaper reports call attention to the spectacular nature of the battles through techniques similar to those we have seen in his novel. In Crane's story of the Rough Riders' "gallant blunder," for example, their noise and bravado appear to be directed more toward making an impression on a domestic audience than toward using effective strategy against the enemy, and in his vivid report of the regulars charging up San Juan Hill, Crane offers the readers cues for cheering, as though he were describing a football game.[36]

If his newspaper reports utilize this cheap telescope, many of Crane's later stories about war test its ramifications and its limits. Much of his late fiction explores the boundary line between action and spectatorship and the consequences of crossing it. The correspondent in "Death and the Child," for example, loses his mind when he tries to step over that line; he takes up arms to join the battle, only to hallucinate that the gun is strangling him. In "The Open Boat," the correspondent finds himself thrust into the role of actor in a classic adventure tale, only to share impotence and blindness with the other men in the boat.

In preparing Crane to view modern wars as spectacles, *The Red Badge of Courage* also taught him the incompatibility of the spectacle with traditional forms of storytelling, a gap only deepened by the newspaper version of the "story," which subordinates narrative context to theatrical effects. The impossibility of narrating experience frames Crane's "War Memories," his fictionalized memoir of the Spanish-American War. "War Memories" opens with a reporter's lament about the difficulty of getting at the "real thing," because, he continues, "war is neither magnificent nor squalid; it is simply life, and an expression of life can always evade us. We can never *tell* life, one to another, although sometimes we think we can" (emphasis added).[37] Yet if "telling" life in a coherent narrative is impossible, displaying it through fragmented scenes structures Crane's retrospective on the war. "War Memories" ends with a procession of wounded soldiers, who parade into town from the battlefield and file past a hotel veranda, "suffering from something which was like stage-fright."[38] Fixing the reader in the position of spectator, the narrator calls attention both to his own theatricality and to its limits as he draws the curtains on the last line: "The episode was closed. And you can depend upon it that I have told you nothing at all, nothing at all, nothing at all."[39] Like Henry's recollection of the battle, Crane's "War Memories" of his activity as a correspondent form a fragmented spectacle, which he refuses to contextualize within the narrative of experience or history.

The link between Crane's revision of the Civil War and his representation of international warfare in the 1890s may help explain the unique position of *The Red Badge of Courage* in literary history, not only as the classic novel about the American Civil War but also as a paradigm of the modern American war novel. The popularity of Crane's book in both England and America in the 1890s can be understood in the context of the heightened militarism in both cultures, enacted on the battlefields of colonial territories. If those British reviewers were correct who read *The Red Badge of Courage* as a critique of jingoism, of the spectatorial lust that facilitated imperial warfare, its critique must be an imminent one that emerges from a narrative structure engaged in producing the spectacle of modern warfare.[40]

In his legacy to the century he did not live to see, Crane not only redefined the war novel through the focus on the psyche of the individual soldier but also "invented the persona of the war correspondent for the novelist" of the twentieth century.[41] The components of this figure who straddles the boundary line between spectator and actor are already present in *The Red Badge of Courage*. There Crane not only outlined a hero and a narrative strategy to be fleshed out by American writers from Ernest Hemingway to Norman Mailer, but his revision of the Civil War also shaped both the experience and the representation of those remote wars that American writers have pursued throughout the twentieth century. It is Crane's anticipation of the modern spectacle of war, more than his historical veracity, that allowed Hemingway to write in 1942 that *The Red Badge of Courage* was the only enduring "real literature of our Civil War."

NOTES

1. Quoted in Charles H. Brown, *The Correspondents' War: Journalists in the Spanish-American War* (New York: Scribners, 1967), p. 1.
2. Stephen Crane, *Reports of War,* ed. Fredson Bowers (Charlottesville: University of Virginia Press, 1971), p. 487.
3. Paul H. Buck, *The Road to Reunion, 1865–1890* (Boston: Little, Brown, 1937), chaps. viii/xi.
4. George Williams, "Lights and Shadows of Army Life," *Century Magazine* 28 (October 1884):810.
5. Editors, *Century Magazine* 28 (October 1884):944.
6. Robert U. Johnson and Clarence C. Buel, eds., *Battle and Leaders of the Civil War,* 4 vols. (New York: The Century Co., 1887–8), preface.
7. Robert A. Lively, *Fiction Fights the Civil War* (Chapel Hill: University of North Carolina Press, 1957), p. 57.

8. Quoted in George M. Fredrickson, *The Inner Civil War: Northern Intellectuals and the Crisis of the Union* (New York: Harper & Row, 1965), p. 170.

9. John Higham, "The Re-Orientation of American Culture in the 1890's," in *Writing American History: Essays in Modern Scholarship* (Bloomington: Indiana University Press, 1970), pp. 73–102.

10. Quoted in Higham, "The Re-Orientation," p. 86.

11. John Berryman, *Stephen Crane* (New York: Meridian Books, 1962), p. 78.

12. On the similarities between naturalism and the romance, see T. J. Jackson Lears, *No Place of Grace: Antimodernism and the Transformation of American Culture, 1880–1920* (New York: Pantheon Books, 1981), pp. 103–7.

13. James D. Hart, *The Popular Book: A History of America's Literary Taste* (1950; rpt. Berkeley: University of California Press, 1963), chap. 11.

14. Quoted in Larzer Ziff, *The American 1890's* (Lincoln: University of Nebraska Press, 1966), p. 265.

15. Lears, *No Place of Grace*, chap. 3.

16. William Dean Howells, "The New Historical Romances," *North American Review* 171 (December 1900):935–6.

17. David Axeen, " 'Heroes of the Engine Room': American 'Civilization' and the War with Spain," *American Quarterly* 36 (Fall 1984):481–502.

18. Theodore Roosevelt, *The Strenuous Life: Essays and Addresses* (New York: The Century Co., 1900) pp. 1–21.

19. Stephen Crane, "Roosevelt's Rough Rider's Loss Due to A Gallant Blunder," New York *World*, June 25, 1898, reprinted in Crane, *Reports of War*, p. 146.

20. Seymour Dodd, *The Song of the Rappahannock* (New York: Dodd, Mead, 1898).

21. Eric Solomon, *Stephen Crane: From Parody to Realism* (Cambridge, Mass.: Harvard University Press, 1966), pp. 1–18.

22. R. W. Stallman and Lillian Gilkes, *Stephen Crane: Letters* (New York: New York University Press, 1960), p. 17.

23. These examples were pointed out by Kenneth Haltman in an unpublished paper.

24. In an 1896 *New York Times* review of *The Red Badge of Courage*, Harold Frederic suggests that this sense of an urban environment structures our reading experience when he compares the characters to strangers on a train: "not a word is expended on telling where they come from, or who they are. They pass across the picture, or shift from one posture to another in its moving composition, with the impersonality of one's

chance fellow-passengers in a railroad car." Harold Frederic, "Review," *New York Times,* January 26, 1986. Reprinted in *Stephen Crane: The Critical Heritage,* ed. Richard Weatherford (London: Routledge & Kegan Paul, 1973), p. 117.

25. General Alexander C. McClurg, letter to the *Dial,* April 16, 1896; rpt. in Weatherford, *Stephen Crane,* pp. 138–41. Donald Pease, "Fear, Rage, and the Mistrials of Representation in *The Red Badge of Courage,*" in Eric Sundquist, ed., *American Realism: New Essays* (Baltimore: Johns Hopkins University Press, 1982), pp. 155–75.

26. Walter Benjamin, "The Storyteller," in *Illuminations,* ed. Hannah Arendt (New York: Schocken Books, 1969), pp. 83–109. Benjamin discusses the challenge presented by the technological and mass qualities of the World War I battlefield to the traditional experience transmitted through stories.

27. Ibid., p. 84.

28. Berryman, *Stephen Crane,* p. 174.

29. J. A. Hobson, *Imperialism: A Study* (1902; reprinted Ann Arbor: University of Michigan Press, 1972), p. 215.

30. Phillip Knightley, *The First Casualty: From Crimea to Vietnam: The War Correspondent as Hero, Propagandist and Myth Maker* (New York: Harcourt, Brace, Jovanovich, 1975), p. 42.

31. Frank Luther Mott, *American Journalism: 1690–1960* (New York: 1962), p. 529.

32. Higham, "The Re-Orientation," p. 84.

33. Crane, *Reports of War,* pp. 487, 492, 495.

34. Stephen Crane, *The Third Violet and Active Service,* ed. Fredson Bowers (Charlottesville: University Press of Virginia, 1976), p. 172.

35. Axeen, "'Heroes of the Engine Room,'" pp. 499–510.

36. Crane, *Reports of War,* pp. 146, 154–65.

37. Stephen Crane, "War Memories," in *Wounds in the Rain* (1900), reprinted in *Tales of War,* ed. Fredson Bowers (Charlottesville: University Press of Virginia, 1970), p. 223.

38. Ibid., p. 263.

39. Op. cit.

40. For examples of this reading, see Weatherford, ed., *Stephen Crane,* pp. 99, 105, 127.

41. Martin Green, *The Great American Adventure* (Boston: Beacon Press, 1984), p. 169.

"He Was a Man"

HOWARD C. HORSFORD

WIDELY familiar novels, like *Tom Jones* or *Emma* or *Great Expectations*, create for us a long-standing and influential tradition of narratives patterned as "education," as growth and development. No inherent necessity requires these accounts of maturation to end in self-knowledge, resolution, and responsible adulthood, but they commonly do. For Tom Jones or Emma Woodhouse this becomes a happy consummation; for the Pip of Dickens's novel, it is also a greater, but in his case a sadder, wisdom. A specialized version of such an influential pattern has been called the "realistic war novel" – Tolstoy's *Sebastopol* (1854–5, translated 1887) is offered as the early example. With this, so it has been argued, there was "established a new generic plot convention: growth from cowardice and inexperience to courage and manhood."[1]

The seemingly direct statements of Henry Fleming's state of mind at the end of Crane's *The Red Badge of Courage*, particularly in its original book form (1895), would appear to be in this vein. Together with the expectations that have accrued with so powerful a novelistic tradition, these statements make it easy to understand why the large majority of readers has so understood the implications of Fleming's two days in battle. Even if a few perceptive readers were rueful in noting the relative cost of young Henry's sensitivity, a regretful depersonalization, they could still accept the thesis of transformation.[2]

Some, however, have found apparent contradictions and discrepanies between these concluding assertions in Fleming's thought regarding his gained maturity and the pervasive irony that hitherto has undercut his mind's working. For these readers the

ending displays a degree of confusion, or at least fictional inepti-
tude, on Crane's part. But especially as a longer manuscript version of the novel has become known, still others read the novel to
the end as a more or less consistently ironic treatment of Fleming's
illusions, rationalizations, and self-justifications.

Let me say at once that I align myself with this last group of
readers, but I would do so in any case, whether one accepts the
originally published version or the manuscript as the more nearly
authoritative. True, passages in the manuscript that reflect the
metaphysical skepticism of Crane's poetry and later stories make
his ironies more emphatic (though turgid writing suggests reasons
why he may have excised these passages at one or more later
stages of revision). Nevertheless, careful attention to the movement of either version of the novel authenticates a reader's skepticism regarding Fleming's concluding self-satisfaction.

Apart from Fleming's insistent preoccupation with self-image,
to himself and in the eyes of others, the only other thing that is
constant throughout the novel is constant alteration: in the endlessly repetitive movement of Fleming's thinking through self-
doubt, self-gratulation, self-excusing, self-abasement, and around
again; in the fundamentally irrational nature of his contradictory
actions, never consciously willed; and in the self-deceiving rationalizations he constructs after the fact. Once this insistently
pervasive pattern of change is acknowledged, it is hard, if not
impossible, to see his concluding self-contemplation as constitut-
ing any reliable finality. These paragraphs come to seem no more
substantial, authentic, and final than any that have preceded. The
novel, and Fleming's fictional life, simply stop at this point, open-
ended and inconclusive.

Of course, this is not to find Crane scorning the real terror of an
inexperienced youth thrust into the murderous chaos of battle.
Nor does this mean to suggest sneering at his frenzied (if limited
and finally meaningless) achievements the second day, which his
fellows and therefore he take to be heroism. If truth resides in
what works, as William James declared, then in that sense Fleming's battle fury can appear heroic. But it is also as mindless as his
first day's flight. In the world of human irrationality that Crane
conceives, of action not consciously volitional, praise is fundamentally as irrelevant as blame or condemnation.

Still less is this meant to ignore Crane's depiction of human behavior, together with the context of its activity, as at once radically absurd yet occasion for pathos. Surely this is what we remember in his most famous short story from two years later, "The Open Boat"; the correspondent comes at last to reflect on the absurdity of imputing any meaning or purpose to the world. In the world of nature, man is a particle of no consequence barely afloat on the monstrous waves. As the men at last flounder through pounding surf to the Florida beach, Billie the oiler, patient and self-sacrificing in the bone-weary rowing against the winter storm, who is strongest and the best swimmer, is meaninglessly drowned. From any cosmic viewpoint, the fate of the four men adrift is purely a matter of indifference; such meaning as the occasion may have resides only in what they have come to feel for each other. In this view, the image of the four in the fragile little boat amid purposeless but monstrously dangerous nature becomes a haunting image of the general human condition.

In other stories, that simply nonrational world (as in the death of Billie) parallels the recurrent irrationality of man. Crane's sense of this in behavior under stress is sometimes expressed in a comic moment, as for example when the man in "The Monster" frantically tears off shutters from the burning house. At other times, the comic is rather grimly ironic. In "A Mystery of Heroism," the soldier, Collins, has been challenged on a dare and goaded into going for water in the midst of a vicious fire fight; but there he finds himself among the flying shells without knowing why, and in the event, the bucket he brings back is accidentally, meaninglessly spilled by two frivolous young officers.

Among these stories written after *The Red Badge of Courage*, "The Blue Hotel" is particularly remarkable for the sense of irrational behavior, of grotesque absurdity ending in grim fatality. The Swede from the East, believing much too much in the dime-novel tales of Western violence, in manic excitement challenges a player for cheating in a petty card game. They, along with others, go out into a night of a driving, high-Western-plains blizzard to fight. It makes a powerful image, viewed as if from a rather distant height: Two little men flounder at each other in a lee area free of snow while a fitful lantern flares in the darkness, meagerly lighting up the others who watch while the blizzard's wind howls over their heads. Afterward, the triumphant Swede makes his way through the drifts to the saloon, where his braggart elation will bring on his death; meanwhile, Crane cannot resist inserting his well-known authorial comment:

> We picture the world as thick with conquering and elate humanity, but here, with the bugles of the tempest pealing, it was hard to imagine a peopled earth. One viewed the existence of man then as a marvel, and conceded a glamour of wonder to these lice which were caused to cling to a whirling, fire-smote, ice-locked, disease-stricken, space-lost bulb. The conceit of man was explained by this storm to be the very engine of life. One was a coxcomb not to die in it. (Section VIII)

In a post-Darwinian era, we can of course expect Crane to use the imagery of animal violence for fighting (as he does constantly in the novel): Here in the short story, examples include "leonine cruelty," "ferocious, brutish," crashing together "like bullocks." Nevertheless, the underlying conception that haunts this story, like the rest of Crane's thinking, is not primarily evolutionary and biological, but the physics of Clausius, Lord Kelvin, and Willard Gibbs – the world as sheer energy whose entropy postulates its end as only a stony clinker lost in final darkness. Viewed from such a detached perspective, the antics of these men in the story seem profoundly absurd, yet also ruefully pathetic.

So also with *The Red Badge of Courage*. In an expansive version of the underlying metaphor of "The Open Boat," the novel begins with a remote, depersonalized view of the armies. Unindividualized masses, denominated only by the color of their uniforms, wait to engage once more in murderous violence, while all about and far beyond this little cockpit of war, impersonal nature goes on with its business of burgeoning spring. Repeatedly throughout this short novel, we are recalled to this encompassing context: nature indifferent to the chaotic violence where, in smoky obscurity, ignorant armies clash by day and night is filled with imagined monstrous terrors.

Three or four quick examples are characteristic. As the regiment advances toward battle (in Chap. 2) like "long serpents" crawling from hill to hill, we are reminded that "the sky over-head was of a fairy blue." Later, as they come closer to the battle line, Fleming, with intensified vision, sees that "these battalions . . . were woven red and startling into the gentle fabric of softened greens and browns. It looked to be a wrong place for a battle-field." Still again, during a respite in the second morning's skirmishing, the narrative continues to contrast man's destructive activity with nature's tranquility: "A cloud of dark smoke as from smouldering ruins went up toward the sun now bright and gay in the blue, enamelled sky" (Chap. 18/17). In the next to last chapter, a similar contrast describes the final charge as "a blind and despairing rush by the collection of men in dusty and tattered blue, over a green sward and under a sapphire sky." But the passage most often quoted comes after the first inconclusive engagement, as Fleming looks around with

> a flash of astonishment at the blue pure sky and the sun-gleamings on the trees and fields. It was surprising that nature had gone tranquilly on with her golden processes in the midst of so much devilment. (Chap. 5)

Those who have seen the film John Huston made of Crane's novel may remember how Huston and his cameraman capitalized on this double perspective. Especially in the battle scenes, the camera alternated between close attention to the principal actors and panning surveys of the battlefield as if from a distant height; in the event, the movement of men, the rush of flags, the flash of guns in the obscuring smoke became seemingly minuscule irruptions against the spring countryside. Here, in the opening of the novel, we have the equivalent of a camera, slowly panning in from a great distance, impersonally visualizing armies as indistinguishable masses, but gradually bringing into focus nearly anonymous, nearly characterless figures who are personalized only by some simple adjective – "tall," "loud," "fat," "young." Only after a while, as the requirements of dialogue mandate, do a few begin to have names: Jim Conklin, Wilson, and finally, after several pages, Henry Fleming. (It is worth recalling that in the manuscript, Crane removed as many as he could of such proper names originally written in.)

Insistently, the "youthful private" remains the "youth" in his adolescent preoccupation with self-image. That is early evident in his recollections of his daydreams of flaming heroism, couched in schoolboy Homeric and chivalric terms but somehow without pain and blood. The preoccupation with self, through all his alternations of mood and attitude, is his most distinguishing attribute, and even when he seems to come closest to some sort of just self-estimation, it is immediately qualified in an overriding concern for the appearance he can make to others.

In Crane's representation, Fleming is not so much a conventionally developed character, with a stable and distinct central being, as a welter of conflicting subjective sensations — an aspect of what Conrad first called Crane's "impressionism." But like so much else in the novel, this subjectivism also has alternative states: a subjective, hence narrow "impressionism" and an equally subjective "expressionism," a projection of wish, fear, terror on the external world.[3]

The sense in which the derivative adjective "impressionistic" is being used here can be illustrated by an event on the regiment's march toward battle. After the long, restless season in winter quarters, filled with baseless rumors, the men at last move out, starting and stopping in the fashion that a later generation called "hurry up and wait." Then suddenly, in early dawn, they are rushed half-awake toward the front line. With vivid clarity, Henry sees ahead not the battle scene he had imagined but "little fields girted and squeezed by a forest . . . knots and waving lines of skirmishers . . . running hither and thither and firing at the landscape" (Chap. 3). Then the marching troops come upon a dead soldier in a Confederate uniform, lying in the road (a telling moment in Fleming's initiation, by the way, that Huston emphasized in making the film). But what Fleming's attention seizes upon is the vision of "the soles of his shoes . . . worn to the thinnest of writing-paper and from a great rent in one, the dead foot projected piteously."[4]

This is a subjectively concentrated perception of an objective fact; it is Fleming's first of four personal encounters with death, not at all allowed for in his adolescent imaginings. Elsewhere he projects on the world, usually in expressionistic terms, his subjective wishful thinking or imagined terrors. Probably the most notorious of the occasions in which Fleming's self-excusing becomes a wishful interpretation of the event is his contemplation of the fleeing squirrel (in Chap. 7); here he rationalizes flight as nature's "sign" justifying his own action. For the corollary state of fearful anxiety, Crane risks hyperbolic language (as he frequently does, notably in the scene of burning chemicals in "The Monster"); here it is meant to evoke the feverish but untutored quality of Fleming's imagination. It is the language and imagery of a child's imagination – demons, ogres, dragons: figures of nightmare threat.

In the predawn dark, campfires behind the Confederate lines glow like the red eyes of a row of advancing dragons. Shadows aroused from sleep move like monsters (a recurrent word) in the gloom; the general on horseback, silhouetted against the first dim light, seems gigantic. And as the columns of men begin to move out, they seem to Fleming's anxious consciousness "moving monsters," "huge crawling reptiles" (Chap. 2).

The pervasive animism Crane appears to invest in nature functions to express subjective desire or fears and allied imaginings projected on nature by a youth like Fleming. Yet simultaneously, this feature seems to create an animate life altogether alien and impervious to man. This expressionistic mode so pervades the novel as to determine its overall tonality. The narrative so pervasively embodies this projective expression of Fleming's thinking that all his mental convolutions become the matter of ironic presentation – not by denying the actuality of his terrors or mindless frenzy but by representing his feelings or rationalizations *about* these moments. Almost tediously, such irony is enforced by unremitting juxtaposition, most obviously in the opposition of his successive actions, more subtly and complexly by the unending modulations in his thought.

Constant alternation is indeed the structural principle of the novel, in large movements and small. When the regiment first moves toward the front line (in Chap. 3), the men occupy successively three different positions before noon; yet in the afternoon, they return back over the same ground, having been "marched from place to place with apparent aimlessness." Throughout, the flags tilt forward, then back, as the regiment charges forward and then retreats, and Fleming and Wilson make a furious, desperate advance, only to be called back. At the end, after the fierce fighting of the second day for what seems in retrospect an astonishingly small advance, "the regiment received orders to retrace its way" and the whole division moves back toward the river they had crossed only a few nights before. And if one knows that Crane had in mind the actual battle of Chancellorsville, it may not be irrelevant to remember that its bloody carnage resulted in nothing gained at all – certainly not for the Union army.

As applied particularly to Fleming, alternation as a principle holds together narratively the otherwise irrational and subjective welter that constitutes him. Overall, it is unmistakably established in the structure of action itself during the two central days of battle. On day one, Fleming first stands and fires mindlessly as the enemy skirmishers are repulsed; then panic-stricken, in equal mindlessness, he flees when the enemy returns. The two halves of the novel then repeat this pattern in reverse. The first half, essentially the day of flight, is counterbalanced by his return in the second half, the day of attributed heroism.

In this way, the elements of the manifest action stand in simple, direct opposition, yet in motivation they are similar in unwilled impulse. The action of Fleming's mind, however, is usually less abrupt in its contrasts. Nevertheless, we as readers are directly initiated early on. As a rural youth (presumably from somewhere in upstate New York), he has despaired of an age so advanced and tamed that epic battle or chivalric heroism have been outmoded; yet the onset of the Civil War (never so named) revives juvenile fantasies, and he burns to enlist. Though his mother sensibly resists, he does enlist, and boyishly delights in the admiration elicited as he struts in his new uniform, imagining the noble deeds he will perform. But the long winter of waiting in camp renews a sense of disillusion, even as, when spring returns with wild rumors of coming battle, he begins to doubt his own untested bravery. Now, as the regiment moves hastily toward the front, he feels coerced, helplessly constrained, with not a hint of awareness of the contradiction.

> But he instantly saw that it would be impossible for him to escape from the regiment. It enclosed him. . . . He was in a moving box.
> As he perceived this fact, it occurred to him that he had never wished to come to the war. He had not enlisted of his free will. He had been dragged by the merciless government. (Chap. 3)

In a paradoxical way, Crane represents his thinking, constantly preoccupied with self, as intensely self-aware, yet his mind is only rarely aware of how self-contradictorily it has moved from moment to moment. On this march to the front lines, he had been fearful that he will flee, but he feels hopelessly trapped. Yet he forgets "many things as he [feels] a sudden impulse of curiosity" that becomes a deep preoccupation when they pass by the dead Confederate; but curiosity ceases and "absurd ideas" take hold. He imagines that the unfamiliar landscape threatens, that shadows are formidable; the officers are fools, and they will all be sacrificed. He feels a duty to harangue his fellows, to convince them to flee slaughter; but then he thinks that this is hopeless because they will not listen. He begins to lag, feeling "tragic" self-pity until the lieutenant with "insolent" words and the flat of his sword hurries him up − a "mere brute" with no "appreciation of fine minds."

Almost from moment to moment, his mind veers from one tack to another; nothing seems stable or coherently developed in his thought. Presently, it occurs to him that, reputedly, man changes in battle, and he becomes feverishly impatient for the event that will still his uncertainties. As the regiment's seemingly pointless movements wear the day away, all his earlier doubts are magnified; he comes to think that death might be welcome, a respite from his vexations and his overwhelming anxieties. But the outbreak of the first fire fight (in Chap. 4) briefly paralyzes him: As he sees others running, he believes he would, too, if he could just get control of his legs. The company captain repeatedly shouts at the men not to fire until ordered, but Fleming at this point cannot even remember if his gun is loaded. In a kind of hysterical automatism:

> Before he was ready to begin, before he had announced to himself that he was about to fight, he threw the obedient, well-balanced rifle into position and fired a first wild shot. Directly, he was working at his weapon like an automatic affair.
>
> He suddenly lost concern for himself. . . . He became not a man but a member. . . . For moments, he could not flee no more than a little finger can commit a revolution from a hand. (Chap. 5)

What is particularly emphasized in this account, we observe, is its quality of being altogether mindless. Fleming is filled with a "red rage," like that of a "pestered animal." "His impotency appeared to him and made his rage into that of a driven beast."

But now, when the attack seems repulsed, his fury recedes, and he goes "into an ecstasy of self-satisfaction" (Chap. 6). He perceives himself and his fighting as "magnificent." "He felt that he was a fine fellow. . . . He smiled in deep gratification." Yet it is just at this moment that the attack is renewed. With remarkable prescience, Crane attributes to Fleming the frenzied responses that modern brain researchers know as a panic attack, the brain chemistry of the fight-or-flight reaction. In the event, Fleming reacts both ways in quick succession. The sudden onset of the first attack had produced a kind of mindless counterresponse. The apparent success of the repulse then generates complacency regarding the fear that had seemed to disappear, and the feeling of release from the chaotic violence that at last was over and done with. But no — with a kind of mad, baffling iteration, it all has to be faced again.

With equal plausibility but equally frantic mindlessness, Fleming now flees: "It was an onslaught of redoubtable dragons." He yells with fright, turns, and becomes (in a worn simile) "like a proverbial chicken" — the kind of frantic movement that does not know its own direction. "He ran like a blind man," with the "zeal of an insane sprinter." Insofar as he is thinking at all, he believes that everyone is in imminent danger of annihilation: The gunners who continue their methodical firing are merely stupid machines; he *knows* the officer trying to force his horse to the front will soon be dead. The men of the brigade moving to reinforce the line are uncomprehending fools, and he *knows* the whole line must retreat or be destroyed. But the line holds (Chap. 6), and in bitterness, Fleming thinks himself betrayed, wronged by *their* "imbecile" stupidity (Chap. 7).

Now he enters on a torrent of self-pity, justifying the wisdom of *his* "enlightened" action in contrast to the universal stupidity. In his self-righteous anger against them, "he knew it could be proven that they had been fools." But irrepressibly, his concern for self-justification becomes, as always, concern for how he will appear to others. He imagines the derision of his fellows when he returns as an excessive punishment for inconsequential guilt, and he pities himself "acutely."

All of these endless later fluctuations in consciousness take place within probably little more than an hour since the beginning of the first engagement. Notoriously, they continue on through his fatuous self-excusing by invoking benevolent nature as he moves farther away from the sounds of battle. "The landscape gave him assurance. A fair field, holding life. It was the religion of peace. It would die if its timid eyes were compelled to see blood. He conceived nature to be a woman with a deep aversion to tragedy" (Chap. 7).

In reading the flight of the squirrel as a wise commentary on his own behavior – "Nature had given him a sign" – he ignores the meaning of the small feral animal pouncing on a fish. That is, until in one of the two or three most notable scenes in the novel, he pushes into the serenity of the chapellike grove, only to confront the scarifying sight of the corpse, putrefying and overrun by ants. In the manuscript, the passage specifying the horrified reversal of his feelings about nature has been canceled, but the implications are unmistakable in any event.

In similar ways, the whole of the novel embodies this strategy of alteration and reversal. What the novel enforces, then, whether in the shortened version of the published book or in the manuscript, is this pervasive unreliability of Fleming's ideas about himself and his actions. Whatever he thinks at one moment, whatever he asserts to himself he "knows," is directly undercut a few sentences or a few paragraphs later.

Certain other observations are also critical, one suggested by the shattering encounter just noted. In his adolescent daydreams of battle, such affairs had been "vague and bloody conflicts that had thrilled him with their sweep and fire. In visions, he had seen himself in many struggles. He had imagined peoples secure in the shadow of his eagle-eyed prowess" (Chap. 1). Notably absent in such vague imaginings is any sense of the specifics of death. Only when the advancing troops first come upon the dead Confederate does this begin to seize his obsessive attention. Now here, in isolation, he sees one of his own nameless compatriots, the blue uniform faded to green, the staring dead-fish eyes, the yellow mouth, and the appalling ants.

Shocking as this confrontation is, there is another much more personal one to come. When he joins the line of the wounded straggling to the rear, he discovers his sometime hut-mate and friend, Jim Conklin, the "tall" soldier, just in time to watch the hideous process of his dying. The death convulsions of a wounded animal – a rabbit, a squirrel, a raccoon – the jerkings and twitchings are here those of a man. Like such an animal, Conklin seeks a covert in which to die:

> Finally, the chest of the doomed soldier began to heave with a strained motion. It increased in violence until it was as if an animal was within and was kicking and tumbling furiously to be free. . . .
> Suddenly, his form stiffened. . . . Then it was shaken by a prolonged ague. . . .
> . . . For a moment, the tremor of his legs caused him to dance a sort of hideous horn-pipe. His arms beat wildly about his head. . . .

and he falls, bouncing a little way from the earth, to become simply an "It" with a ghastly grin lying still in the grass (Chaps. 9 and 10).

The tattered soldier exclaims "Gawd" in some kind of wonderment, but Fleming turns in "livid rage" toward the battlefield with an aborted "Hell – " Thereafter, in Crane's finely honed phrasing, "He now thought that he wished he was dead" (Chap. 10 and again, after another series of reversals, in Chap. 11). Yet in his own intense self-absorption, he later thinks of his friend only once; to Wilson he merely mentions Conklin's death, briefly and unemotionally. And in his last direct encounter with an individual's end, that of the Confederate flag bearer in the next-to-last chapter, though the descriptive details are much the same as with Conklin, the tone of his reaction is curiously detached. By such a standard, no doubt, one could argue that he has begun to be hardened and desensitized by experience; by that dubious standard, he is indeed a "better soldier."

His self-absorption when he is returned to his regiment, dazed and faint, is understandable enough but not very admirable in his petty irritation with Wilson's awkward kindness. So another kind of contrast is reinforced here, a kind of contrast that began with Conklin's more mature equanimity in the face of uncertainty during their first approach to battle (Chap. 3). Wilson, the loud soldier, now appears to be chastened and tempered by the day's events, but Fleming remains the perennial self-centered "youth" – the more emphatically for the changes Crane made in the manuscript to isolate and highlight this quality.

That self-absorption should doubtless not be confused with what we ordinarily call selfishness, but it approaches that state in his notorious treatment of the badly wounded and tattered soldier. Stumbling along with the file of the injured, the uninjured Fleming morosely wishes he too had some public sign justifying his presence among the retreating. But to Fleming, without a "little red badge of courage," the tattered soldier's well-meant query, "Where yeh hit," is consternating, and he slinks away. Later when the tattered man reappears at the scene of Conklin's death, he himself is weakening, and even as he expresses reiterated concern for Fleming's nonexistent wound, he pathetically speaks of his own need for help. But the renewed question exasperates Fleming's guilty feelings and he turns away angrily, leaving the other to wander helplessly, apparently to die also (Chap. 10).

Near the end, when this memory returns to Fleming, he mentally cringes. But as with the memory of flight, he is able to put it "at a distance" because, characteristically, he can reassure himself at such moments of temporary self-accusation that nobody else knows. Here, as elsewhere, his conception of self rests on various kinds of deception, both of himself and of others. It follows, then, that the central irony of the title is created by his assertion of two outright lies to his fellow soldiers when he is returned to his company.

The contusion from the blow on his head, made by the rifle of a panic-stricken Union soldier, he twice tells Wilson, resulted because he was "shot." And twice, he glibly claims he "got separated" from the unit in the terrible fighting, thereby intending to forestall the gibes and accusations he imagines others might level at him. By so doing, he means to imply that he has been trying to get back ever since. But the plain truth, of course, is that intention had nothing to do with it; entirely passive, he was simply led there by the unknown cheerful soldier. Insofar as Fleming had any intention at all in his dazed state, like Conklin it was only to get out of the way of trampling men, the "dangers and mutilations if he should fall upon the field. . . . He imagined secluded spots where he could fall and be unmolested." "He held continuous arguments as to whether he should lie down and sleep at some near spot, or force himself on until he reached a certain haven" (Chap. 13/12). When the cheery soldier takes charge of him, Fleming is merely "woodenly" passive. When Fleming is at last left standing at the edge of the firelight of his unit's bivouac, he dully fears the ridicule of the men and thinks of slinking off into the darkness to hide, but exhaustion, pain, and hunger drive him to seek comfort: "His ailments, clamoring, forced him to seek the place of food and rest, at whatever cost" (Chap. 14/13).

Recuperated after a night's sleep in Wilson's blanket, Fleming awakens irritable and self-defensive, but complacent as long as he can keep the truth hidden. Despite his friend's well-meant concern, Fleming intends to put him on the defensive to forestall the discovery of the lies. He still has the letters Wilson had entrusted to him in a mawkish moment the day before, and he now regards them as a "weapon," rejoicing that he can be the "master" in any potentially threatening situation. He feels "immensely superior," and condescends to and patronizes his friend. Still later, when Wilson, in some embarrassment, asks for the letters, Fleming intends to make some smart, biting comment, but failing to think of one, instead congratulates himself on his forbearance (Chap. 16/15).

Meanwhile, with his lies undiscovered, he preens himself on his "manhood"; "since nothing could now be discovered, he did not shrink from an encounter with the eyes of judges, and allowed no thoughts of his own to keep him from an attitude of manfulness. He had performed his mistakes in the dark, so he was still a man." Surely, then, the nearly identical phrase at the end of the last chapter should give us skeptical pause. Correspondingly, though others had fled with "terror-struck faces," "he had fled with discretion and dignity." Now he feels "competent to return home and make the hearts of the people glow with stories of war. He could see himself in a room of warm tints telling tales to listeners. He could exhibit laurels." If they "were insignificant; still, in a district where laurels were infrequent, they might shine." "He saw his gaping audience picturing him as the central figure in blazing scenes."

This is the stuff of his prior adolescent fantasies. In fact, however, the events of the second day's battle do offer some ground for a later exhibition of laurels. Some — but perhaps more modest than his subsequent retailed stories will claim. When Fleming becomes briefly modest, it is out of fear of discovery, not genuine self-estimation. As the regiment moves toward the renewed battle, Fleming bitterly complains that though he and the regiment fight like the devil, incompetent generals lose the results. When a sarcastic fellow challenges him for sounding as if he fought yesterday's battle all by himself, Fleming is consternated at the possible sly reference to his fleeing. It is not such a reference, but Fleming becomes "suddenly a modest man" (Chap. 17/16).

As for "heroism," although it is of course true that on this second day of fighting, he stands rather than flees, and even charges forward under conditions that make his — and Wilson's — actions appear bravely heroic, nevertheless it is with no more conscious, willed intention than his panic-stricken running the day before. Blind rage and blind fear share the common characteristic. Fleming loses a "sense of everything but his hate." He is "not conscious that he [is] erect upon his feet." He has felt that he and his fellows deserve some repose for their efforts yesterday. Yet here are the rebels relentlessly attacking again, and in enraged frustration, he crouches and snarls like a cornered animal. And afterward, in a tellingly passive construction, "It was revealed to him that he had been a barbarian, a beast." In still another significant construction, "he was now *what he called* a hero. And he had not been aware of the process" (Chap. 18/17; italics added).

Adjectives, phrases, and sentences can be piled up to emphasize the point. When the unit is ordered to charge (Chap. 20/19), Fleming is "unaware of the machinery of orders that started the charge." He looks "insane." Running, he is "unconsciously in advance" of his fellows. He, like the others, is described as possessed by a "mad enthusiasm," "heedless and blind," and he is puzzled afterward, when he has time again to think, regarding the "reasons he could have had for being there." Still later, when this charge has faltered and fallen back, then resumed with Fleming now the bearer of the talisman flag (Chap. 23/22), his consciousness is that of a "deeply absorbed . . . *spectator*" (italics added); prattling words spew from him "unconsciously," and he is wholly unaware even of breathing. Otherwise, he feels in himself "the daring spirit of a savage, religion-mad," in the grip of his "wild battle-mad" (Chap. 24/23).

Unrelentingly, Crane persists in the process of undercutting or setting in contrast Fleming's successive postures. Occasionally, Crane does allow him to have glimpses of a more proper estimate of his achievements – for example, when he and Wilson hear their unit called "mule-drivers," "New eyes were given to him. And the most startling thing was to learn suddenly that he was very insignificant" (Chap. 19/18). But once again, he immediately makes the general statement into one of personal application, and moreover, so far as any dependable advance in self-perception may seem to have occurred, we might remember that this has happened before, with no permanent access of modesty. After his horrified retreat from the corpse in the woods, for example, he had similarly thought about the fighting from which he fled: "Reflecting, he saw a sort of humor in the point of view of himself and his fellows. . . . They had taken themselves and the enemy very seriously and had imagined that they were deciding the war." (There was also an equivalent passage later canceled at the end of the manuscript's Chap. 15).

We note with no surprise, then, another repetition of much the same pattern. The abortive charge of Chapter 22/21 falters, and the unit falls back. In the overwhelming excitement of movement, the distances traversed had seemed great, but Fleming now sees that they were very small, and he thinks that those "distances, as compared with the brilliant measurings of his mind, were trivial and ridiculous." But this recognition hardly limits his conception of self. "However, to the youth there was a considerable joy in musing upon his performances during the charge. He had had very little time, previously, in which to appreciate himself, so that there was now much satisfaction in quietly thinking of his actions." Of course, the point is not just to deride Fleming's juvenility but to recognize that no single statement expressing his state of mind is ever really final; one can only rely on the factor of his unremitting self-regard, his irrepressible need to think well of himself.

So now, as the regiment falls back in the last chapter, when

Fleming exclaims with satisfaction, "Well, it's all over," we do not even need to keep in mind the actual prolonged defeat at Chancellorsville and the weary onward course of the war. We need recall only his similar feeling after the first skirmish the preceding day. When his mind resumes "its accustomed course of thought," then, the wary reader by now ought to be sufficiently skeptical of any seeming finality. True, among the acts that he reviews in memory are, first, his previous day's flight, and, more reproachfully, the "dogging memory of the tattered soldier, he, who gored by bullets and faint for blood, had fretted concerning an imagined wound in another . . . he who blind with weariness and pain had been deserted in the field." Just as clearly, nevertheless, Fleming is capable of repressing these memories in order to rejoice in what others think of him, his "public image":

> . . . the youth, regarding his procession of memory, felt gleeful and unregretting, for, in it, his public deeds were paraded in great and shining prominence. Those performances which had been witnessed by his fellows marched now in wide purple and gold, hiding various deflections. . . . He spent delightful minutes viewing the gilded images of memory. (Chap. 25/24)

What chiefly concerns him about the painful part of memory is not its justness but whether the fact will become known:

> For an instant, a wretched chill of sweat was upon him at the thought that he might be detected in the thing . . .
> . . . this vision of cruelty brooded over him. It . . . darkened his view of the deeds in purple and gold. . . . He looked stealthily at his companions feeling sure that they must discern in his face evidences . . .
> . . . He saw his vivid error and he was afraid it would stand before him all of his life. (Chap. 25/24)

But as he looks at his weary fellows, it is only with the fear "that they were seeing his thoughts and scrutinizing each detail of the scene with the tattered soldier."

Inasmuch as others do not know, he is gradually able "to put the sin at a distance" and resume musing about himself with complacent satisfaction. He now thinks he feels "a quiet manhood, non-assertive but of sturdy and strong blood. He knew that he would no more quail before his guides wherever they should point. He had been to touch the great death and found that, after all, it was but the great death" (Chap. 25/24). Like Fleming, one might make much of this tautology, but that is to forget the two dramatic scenes so compellingly described, the hideous process of Conklin's dying and death's aftermath, the appalling corpse in the woods.

Fleming may feel assurance in his quiet manhood, and he "knows" he will not again quail, but he has been similarly positive before when it served his need, notably when he fled: He *knew* the battle was lost, he *knew* it could be proven that all who did not flee were fools, he *knew* that any who advanced rather than retreated were as good as dead. If he is convinced (in the third last paragraph) that "He was a man," well – so he had also felt earlier that morning just because "He had performed his mistakes in the dark" (Chap. 16/15).

Certainly, Fleming has undergone a kind of development in the course of these two days, having at the very least been through traumatic experiences. Certainly, he has acquired a few chastening memories, such as his desertion of the tattered soldier. But whether the figure Crane has presented would, in his further life, make anything constructive from those experiences is doubtful in the extreme. It is well, no doubt, to learn to forgive oneself for irremediable errors, but self-forgiveness does not mean simple repression. Where is the acknowledgment of his desertions in a way that would really count for Fleming?[5] What construction for a future does he make of his memory (other than to feel "competent to return home and make the hearts of the people glow with stories of war," thereby to "exhibit laurels")? Inasmuch as these gratifying anticipations had been felt earlier, just after waking from his previous day's flight, surely nothing during the day has modified the self-satisfaction he now feels in those "deeds in purple and gold" publicly witnessed, however mindlessly performed.

The Henry Fleming that Crane presents thus stands in contradistinction to the Fleming many readers have accepted, who take him at his word in these last paragraphs. When we recognize his irrepressible self-regard, however, his desire to create appearance in disregard or suppression of actuality, his irrational behavior in fact, however rationalized afterward, and the utter impermanence of any resolved state of mind, we can view him with a certain detachment and see him as a figure of rueful absurdity. True, he is also a figure of some pathos, certainly not one of contempt, but to the very end Crane presents him with wry irony. Fleming may believe, as the Union army retreats from Chancellorsville, that it is "over." He can believe that the sultry nightmare is past and he is free now to relish images of tranquil skies, fresh meadows, cool brooks, an existence of soft and eternal peace. Would that it were so – for him – for every young man.

NOTES

1. Steven Mailloux, *"The Red Badge of Courage* and Interpretive Conventions: Critical Response to a Maimed Text," *Studies in the Novel* 10 (Spring 1978):48–63; see p. 50.
2. For example, Frederick C. Crews, Introduction to *The Red Badge of Courage* (Indianapolis: Bobbs-Merrill, 1964), p. xx.
3. In an attempt to forestall confusion here, let me say that I am using the terms "impressionism" and "expressionism" more loosely than the narrower senses associated with the history of art, especially painting. I mean only to distinguish broadly between passages that articulate the contents of Fleming's subjectively narrow *perception,* and, conversely, his projection on the external world of the quality or terminology of his subjective *feelings.*
4. As another illustration of working meaning here, one might cite in Chap. 3 of *Maggie,* Crane's first novel, little Jimmie Johnson, sent with a tin pail to the saloon for beer, seeing just hands reaching down over the bar for the pail and pennies, then returning the full pail. Similarly, in the famous opening lines of "The Open Boat," the men see only the color of the winter sea, too preoccupied with danger to dare look up at the sky, which as well might disturb the fragile stability of the tiny dinghy.
5. The later short story, in which an elderly Fleming acknowledges his panic, is, of course, nothing to the point of this novel.

6

Ill Logics of Irony

CHRISTINE BROOKE-ROSE

Some interpretive conventions

All these conflicting interpretations of *Red Badge*'s two texts suggest
that irony resides not in the text (whether in a sentence or a whole
chapter) but in the critic's interpretive conventions.

—Steven Mailloux

WHAT I propose to show is how unstable are the major
concepts in *The Red Badge of Courage* — how they de-
construct themselves as we read so that the irony, which has been
the element most resistant to new modes of understanding this
text, is bound to be unstable. Four major oppositions include *the
hero/the monster, running to/running from, separation/membership,*
and *spectator/spectacle,* all of which are intertwined with each other
and caught up in the opposition that subsumes them — that of
courage/cowardice. The whole of that deconstructive swallowing act
is itself part of a more basic *in/out* opposition that comes into play
in the outsideness or the insideness of the author. "Irony," in
other words, operates throughout the narrative.

Many critics who have disagreed about Crane's irony take the
term "irony" for granted, usually in two ways: They evaluate it
positively, assuming that the author's attitude toward his character
must be clear; and they do not go into its technique. The positive
evaluation of irony has been questioned by Sontag (1969) and
Barthes (1970), and reversed by Bakhtin (1929a), for whom irony
is on the side of "monological" discourse.[1] However complex the
viewpoints in such discourse, the author is always in control and
has the last word on his characters. By contrast, "dialogical" discourse presents the hero as always resisting the voices that try to
determine him, including the author's own ironic perspective. Yet

129

irony, like interpretation, never ends, and even when we watch a character struggle against all definitions of himself, we are still interpreting and still caught in possible ironies.

The techniques involved in irony make it one of the major achievements of the traditional novel by affording us the possibility of being inside someone's mind. One device is known as free indirect discourse, or, as Ann Banfield has renamed it, "Represented Speech and Thought (RST)." The fact that, through misuse, Represented Thought has become a narrative cliché (and has disappeared from serious modern writing) may reflect Barthes's contention that irony too has disappeared, since it represents the power of one discourse over another. But that should not prevent us from analyzing its function in a traditionally ironic text. I shall use the following abbreviations throughout: RT (Represented Thought), NS (Narrative Sentence, i.e. direct from the author), and DD (Direct Discourse, i.e. dialogue between characters). NS/RT will mean an unclear case and NS > RT a Narrative Sentence that turns into Represented Thought.

Distance: Crane and Fleming

> There was a youthful private who listened with eager ears to the words of the tall soldier and to the varied comments of his comrades. (Chap. 1)

The question of viewpoint has too often been taken for granted in the criticism of *Red Badge* and generally assumed to be Henry Fleming's throughout. In fact, two distinct points of view, the author's and the character's, are established from the start. The interpretive convention of filtering scenes through RT demands that the perceiver be described or stated as present.[2] Yet the "youth" is not introduced until after the introductory scenes of the camp at dawn, and when he is, it is an external focalization ("There was a youthful private").

Moreover, the externalized nomination of the youth is maintained throughout, not simply to express the anonymity of the army but to establish the author's voice. It is the author, likewise, who refers to the "loud soldier" and the "tall soldier" (the youth, after all, has known Jim Conklin "since childhood"; Chap. 2).

Names are given only by characters in DD; we learn Henry's first name from his mother in the initial flashback, and his surname appears at the end of Chap. 11, when he imagines what his comrades will say about him in an example of RS. It is technically incorrect, in other words, to say that from the opening paragraph the reader sees through Fleming's eyes, since the reader has not heard of Fleming or even of a youthful private. Indeed, the initial distance is particularly great between the author and the character's represented thoughts, even if RT is occasionally blurred by the ambiguity of the English past tense (as opposed to the imperfect in French).

Yet this distance is far smaller than that between the character's thoughts and his own DD. An obvious analogy can be found in *What Maisie Knew*, about which Henry James explicitly stated that he had represented complex movements in Maisie's development that she herself could not possibly express. The novel presents a particularly interesting use of RST as Maisie's puerile vocabulary is caught up in James's mature syntax. Compared to the youth, however, the childish Maisie is altogether articulate. *Red Badge* never offers DD that might allow us to imagine someone who could possibly think the complex, sophisticated, and metaphoric thoughts attributed to the youth.[3]

This does not mean that he cannot have them, but only that the author is verbalizing his confused impulses for him. Moreover, the very consistency throughout the appellation the "youth" shows that RT is being used for half-conscious or unarticulated thoughts; after all, one rarely calls oneself by an appellation. Two distinct voices appear from the start, then, the first of which is clearly the author's NSs, both descriptive and ironical ("The cold was passing"/"he said pompously"). The author can also tell us that the youth was *unconscious* of something he then proceeds to describe, or what the youth was *later* to think, or that he and his friend had "a geographical illusion concerning a stream" (Chap. 19/18). He can make judgments about the youth's "tupenny fury," (Chap. 10) and see the youth in external focalization: "A scowl of mortification and rage was upon his face" (Chap. 21/20). He can shift to the collective viewpoint of the "men," and with the death of Jim Conklin can even enter into another consciousness: "He was invaded by a creeping strangeness that slowly enveloped him" (Chap. 9).

The other distinct voice is the youth's, whether in RT — first in flashback, then contemporaneously — or in DD. In other words, the really complex movements are either in NS, emphasized by an unusual number of verbs of perception, and where the irony is clear and sometimes heavy; or they are in RT, left to betray themselves in an irony that operates metatextually.

The hero and the monster

Il faut interroger inlassablement les "métaphores."
— Derrida, "La Pharmacie de Platon"

The famous monsters in the novel's opening paragraph, are thus presented unfiltered, direct from the author, though they are metaphorically implied rather than stated. The image of "an army stretched out on the hills" that "awakened" to "cast its eyes" is echoed by another implied monster of liquid mud purling "at the army's feet." Yet a third monster appears on the other side, with "the red, eye-like gleam of hostile campfires set in the low brow of distant hills." Both armies are monsters, neutrally likened to the "brown and green" no man's-land between them. Yet we also soon learn that the youth had chatted across that battleground with an enemy soldier who had called him "a right dum good feller," and that this incident "had made him temporarily regret war" (Chap. 1).

The concept of the hero is treated so soon with irony that it can be considered hardly constructed, let alone deconstructed. The "greeklike" and "Homeric" dreams that appear in the youth's early flashback remind us of the context in which classical heroes appeared. They were invariably great chieftains who had names, who killed other named nobles in individual combat after an exchange of identities and genealogies, and who were often helped *in extremis* by protective gods. There is little sense of an army of common soldiers in Homer, Virgil, or later romances. Moreover, the contrast initially suggested between the traditional hero and the anonymous youth is presented as already in the past: he rapidly forgets them. When these concepts reappear, they are deconstructed not only by the narrative events but, more especially, by the multilevel irony at the end of Chap. 16/15. It is after that incident that the youth imagines himself back home telling war tales to "the consternation and the ejaculations of his mother and the young lady at the seminary. . . . Their vague feminine formula for beloved ones doing brave deeds on the field of battle without risk of life would be destroyed." Part of the irony of this idea of the hero is that it is a man's view of a woman's view, which the text itself denies through both the attitude of the youth's mother and his own impatient disappointment at her.

What then is a hero? In the novel's opening, he is legend in its initial sense of *legenda* (things to read) – what people read about, hear about, and say. And he can only be clearly defined by what he has to fight against – the monster. By Chapter 2, however, the monsters invoked by the text have considerably changed their signifieds. They are no longer two armies lying in wait, nor are they even the enemy, but are instead, parts of the youth's army: "dark shadows that moved like monsters," "crawling *reptiles*," "two *serpents* crawling" (Chap. 2, all NS > RT)

This shift from the initial objective monsters to the youth's fear of his own side occurs partially because he is concerned with "his problem," introduced in Chap. 1, of whether he will run – a "problem" that separates him from the others. He keeps trying to discover whether they too are troubled, and constantly projects his fear onto what "they" will think of him. "They" become the monsters, until, by the end of Chap. 2, "he saw visions of a thousand-tongued fear that would babble at his back and cause him to flee" (RT). After his flight he returns to camp, and "of a sudden he confronted a black and monstrous figure," which turns out to be his friend Wilson (Chap. 14/13, NS/RT). The monster has become not only his own fear projected onto others, but the fear of what they would say that might then cause him to run. Soon the metaphor shifts again: "The youth looked at the men nearest him. . . . They were going to look at war, the red animal, war, the blood-swollen god" (Chap. 3, RT). The identical phrase is repeated in Chap. 13, together with dragons that by then represent the enemy and an image of "the infernal mouth of the war god" (Chap. 6, RT). The adjective "red" is also associated so regularly with war that it can evoke the monster almost by itself: "the red, formidable difficulties of war had been vanquished" (Chap. 6, RT). By the novel's final lines, the identification is clear: "He had rid himself of the red sickness of battle" (RT). From the author's initial monsters we have moved to the character's monsters as (1) elements of his own army, representing (2) his own fear of his comrades' opinion, projected onto (3) war, then (4) the enemy, then reinteriorized as (5) a red sickness (all RT).

After his flight, the dragons seem less terrible: "He had been out among the dragons, he said, and he assured himself that they were not so hideous as he had imagined them. [. . .] A stout heart often defied; and defying, escaped them. And, furthermore, how could they kill him who was the chosen of the gods?" (Chap. 16/15, RT). The dragons have missed him because he ran, and therefore he is a hero. Like other justifications of his flight, this kind of self-betrayal is always depicted in RT. As the tale progresses, however, and as the youth becomes more familiar with the monsters, they get curiously defabulated ("wagons . . . like fat sheep": Chap. 13/12, RT), as does the author's stereotyping comparisons ("dog-like obedience," "wolflike temper," "like a mad horse," "as a panther at prey," (Chaps. 14/13, 20/19, 21/20, 24/23). The army types people, and the author does too, not only as the youth would have seen them ["the officer who rode like a cowboy" (Chap. 19/18, RT)] but in NS: "the colonel's manner changed from that of a deacon to that of a Frenchman" (Chap. 22/21, NS). No more than the phrase "the tall soldier" can this come from the youth.

Thus, the author is theoretically objective, and yet classifies and judges: Both armies are monsters; man is an animal and fights like one. However, the youth whose thought the author represents rehandles every signifier according to his desires and fears. The monster is the youth and is also every man in every army. Every man, including the youth, can be a hero. Yet the monster in the youth that represents his fear of what others will say about his running suggests that cowardice, like heroism, is for the youth what people say about him. The monster and the hero are in fact one.

Running (to and from)

The pitifulest thing out is a mob. That's what an army is — a mob;
they don't fight with courage that's born in them, but with courage
that's borrowed from their mass, and from their officers.
— *Adventures of Huckleberry Finn*

The process of constant shifts and reversals in running resembles
the hero/monster opposition; running away involves separation,
which involves watching and therefore a kind of running to.
Clearly, there are many different kinds of running, but when the
youth considers his "problem" at the beginning, there is only one
meaning: Would he run? Would they run? Would Jim run? When
in Chapter 3 "he found himself running down a wood-road . . .
carried by a mob," running has reversed its meaning: running *to*
battle, *with* men, in a mob (NS > RT). The opposition to/from is
trivial, with the privilege of tradition placed on "to." In practice,
however, the running into battle is not positively valued here, but
wrapped throughout in notions of an inability to do otherwise, of
unconsciousness, of wild and primitive behavior.

There is also a clear distinction made in the treatment of others
running away (handled as objective acts by the narrator or with
scorn by the youth after his flight) and in the treatment of himself
running away (handled first in NS as he yells with fright and turns,
but afterward in RT as a world-shaking event). The description
that "he was like a proverbial chicken. He lost the direction of
safety" shifts to external focalization: "on his face was all the
horror of those things which he imagined. . . . He ran like a blind
man" (Chap. 3). Later, his shame and self-justifications are all in
RT and are too well known to be detailed. I shall merely stress the
shifts in evaluation:

1. *Running from battle:* envisaged with terror (RT/DD), described
   externally (NS), rehandled subjectively (RT), lied about (DD),
   and eventually minimized (RT). Experienced as unconscious,
   animallike, unmanly.

   Running to battle: also experienced as animallike and unmanly (RT and NS), repeated with more and more irony, (NS).
   For instance, (1) "He went instantly forward, like a dog, who,
   seeing his foes lagging, turns and insists on being pursued

(Chap. 18/17, NS) – the "foes" being his own comrades and the dog's behavior normally that of a joyful game with its master; and (2) "he ran desperately as if pursued for a murder" (Chap. 20/19, NS). Here the youth is suddenly a criminal, and his comrades are the police. This is more serious than canine snarls, but both comparisons describe running into battle in terms of flight, as if one were pursued by one's own side.

There are various subtypes, such as running for cover or for an aimed spot (Chaps. 20/19, 24/23, RT); running out of curiosity (Chap. 6, NS); running back to battle after flight; or even running into battle as deliberate walk: "The youth walked stolidly into the midst of the mob, and with his flag" (Chap. 15/14, NS).

2. *Running by others:* described dispassionately and not devalued (NS), although this is witnessed with horror (RT) and sometimes imitated in panic (NS). When he learns on the second day that others of his regiment have also fled, the youth reluctantly decides he is not unique. Yet he now can scorn his fellows, for he had fled with discretion and dignity (Chap. 16/15, RT).

   Running by himself: sometimes mediated in shame, and usually in fear of what others will say (e.g., Chaps. 7, 11); projected onto others (nature, generals, the universe); rehandled as wise strategy; compared favorably with that of others; and in general minimized (RT).

3. *Running from a defeat or from a victory:* "The youth cringed as if discovered at a crime. By heavens, they had won after all" (Chap. 7, NS > RT). The running is made worse by victory, since a defeat would be a "salve," and he later hopes for it as "a roundabout vindication of himself" (Chap. 11, RT).

4. *Running from or toward death:* The horrifying spectacles of the dead soldier and the tattered soldier prompt the youth to flight; elsewhere, death seems preferable to running (Chap. 3, RT) or is desired as personal revenge on the general (Chap. 23/22, RT). More dramatically, he is amazed to see Jim running *to* his death: "Gawd! he's runnin'!" (Chap. 9, DD).

5. *Running as an illusion in space and time:* "His mind flew in all directions" (Chap. 14/13, NS); "He discovered that the distances, as compared with the brilliant measurings of his mind, were trivial and ridiculous" (Chap. 22/21, NS). It soon ceases to be as clear as it was at the beginning in which direction he is running – the most dramatic instance of which occurs when

fleeing troops meet those who have already fled and who are now panicked into returning by a new enemy group (Chap. 21/20, NS).

No doubt other configurations appear, since the word "run" is extremely frequent, along with such equivalents as "sweep," "rush," "scatter," "scamper," and "charge." But the interpretations and hence the irony vary enormously, especially since NS is clearly different from the self-betraying RT. Moreover, all the senses are caught up in the ideas of separateness and spectacle. The youth's running had not been observed, at least as far as he knows, and because unobserved, it ceases to count.[4] In the end, neither author nor character (for different reasons, of course) puts a particularly negative value on running from battle or a positive one on running into battle.

Separateness and membership

Join the army, meet interesting people, and kill them.
—Graffiti

Separateness and membership are not manifestations of the more abstract opposition of absence/presence. Even in the opening chapter, the youth feels separate from his companions while in their presence, and in Chapter 2 he "continually tried to measure himself by his comrades" for traces of fear or courage. Moreover, phrases of separateness are frequent throughout (such as "took no part" and "kept from intercourse with"). This separateness stems both from his fear of being a coward and from the conviction that he is superior. After fighting well for the first time, he even becomes separated from himself: "Standing apart from himself, he viewed the last scene. He perceived that the man who had fought thus was magnificent" (Chap. 6, RT). Nevertheless, because it involves loss of membership, the separation caused by running away is hard to bear. It has to be rehandled, first as a personal affront when he learns that the enemy's attack has been repulsed, then as a condition of his superior wisdom and strategy: "the imbecile line had remained and had become victors" (Chap. 7, RT). His conviction of superiority is particularly strong in the original Chapter 12.

Before this, he is separated through envy, as when he watches a column marching into battle and "felt he was regarding a procession of chosen beings. The separation was as great to him as if they had marched with weapons of flames and banners of sunlight" (Chap. 11, RT). And with the wounded, he wishes he too could have his "little red badge of courage" (Chap. 9, RT). Indeed, his separateness is complex enough to warrant a point-by-point presentation:

1. He fears he is unlike those he believes to be heroes, and although relieved to hear Jim admit he might run, prefers death as a solution (Chap. 1 and Chap. 3, RT).

2. He is brave but in "battlesleep" and part of a mob, having learned that fighting means being "not a man but a member" (Chap. 5, RT).

3. He separates himself by running, so he (a) has been wronged, (b) is superior to those who stayed (Chap. 7, RT).

4. He envies the brave and feels separate, but also envies the wounded, and feels an intruder among the dead (Chaps. 8, RT).

5. He is different from others in being protected by the gods, and his flight is a sign of this (Chap. 16/15, RT).

6. He admits he is one of the unfit, and so wants revenge on the universe (Chap. 12).

7. When he hears that others of the regiment fled, he is at first relieved, but then scorns them and needs to distinguish himself as one who fled "with discretion and dignity" (Chap. 16/15, RT).

This complicated, self-canceling separateness is then reversed in the apparent bravery of the last chapters. Yet even in communal "battlesleep," he effectively reseparates himself by being "not conscious," continuing to use his rifle after everyone has stopped. He realizes that his fellows regard him as a "war-devil" (Chap. 18/17, RT), and soon feels ashamed at having been "a barbarian, a beast" who fought separately and unnecessarily (Chap. 18/17, RT). He remains separate to the last, in fact, not only from his friends but from the author as well (see the section "In and Out: Fleming and Crane").

Spectator and spectacle

Supposing they gave a war, and nobody came.

—Graffitti

All these concepts are caught up in that of the spectacle, since the youth is perpetually the spectator who watches his comrades, the battles, and always himself. Indeed, he often *makes* a spectacle of himself, turning himself into a spectacle even when separated and alone. Crane emphasizes this role by introducing NSs with verbs of perception, so that they shift to RT: "he saw," "he stared," "he observed," "he viewed," "he watched," "he gawked." But the theme is far more explicit than this, as the soldiers constantly become spectacles for each other – whether it is new recruits being mocked by veterans, or cowards being watched by those still advancing, or the youth himself being stared at when he goes on shooting. This pattern is characteristic of the youth, who watches far more than he acts, out of a curiosity that even seems at times to overcome his fear: "he felt an unconscious impulse of curiosity. He scrambled up the bank with a speed that could not be exceeded by a bloodthirsty man. He expected a battle scene" (Chap. 3, NS).

Time after time, when one expects him to have no alternative but to fight, the youth becomes a spectator. Even on one of the rare times when he is said to shoot, he pauses: "He slowly lifted his rifle and catching a glimpse of the thick-spread field he blazed at a cantering cluster. He stopped then and began to peer as best he could through the smoke" (Chap. 6, NS). And during his flight there is much peering, spying, and staring at other units still fighting, which culminates in his horrified, fascinated stare at the dead soldier. Back with his regiment, he watches the soldiers who seem likewise dead but who are only asleep by the fire. When the general calls them "mule-drivers," he and his friend become eavesdroppers, and later, instead of fighting, he runs toward a clump of trees and stares "like an insane soldier. . . . It seemed to the youth that he saw everything" (Chap. 20/19, NS). The spectator/spectacle collocation becomes more complex when he seizes the flag from the dying color bearer. Startled by the sudden troop movements, he first "walked stolidly into the midst of the mob and with the flag in hands . . . unconsciously assumed the attitude of the color-bearer of the preceding day." Then he becomes apparently immobile: "The youth's eyes instantly turned in the direction indicated. . . . [H]e strained his vision to learn . . . and achieved a new unsatisfactory view of the enemy" (Chap. 21/20, NS).

The narrative shift to a collective viewpoint occurs just as the charge is repulsed, and the men "made an ungainly dance of joy at the sight of this tableau" (Chap. 21/20, NS). Although the youth has done nothing, he takes time to "appreciate himself" (Chap. 22/21, NS), and only now do we learn (1) that the general thought the regiment had fought like a lot of mule-drivers (Chap. 22/21, DD, NS) and (2) that the colonel had singled out the youth and his friend for praise. The fact that the reader has not seen this spectacle, but only hears of it secondhand and in comical DD, suggests that it may be wild exaggeration. In the next charge, the youth is still color bearer, but to spite the general he has "resolved not to budge" (Chap. 23/22, RT): "He was deeply absorbed as spectator" (Chap. 23/22, NS). Yet he is galvanized into action by the regiment's weakening defense, and in plunging forward at the enemy flag, he thus becomes a spectacle again (Chap. 23/22, mostly NS). A reversal has taken place in the presentation: In the first action he adopts a heroic pose, then merely sits and watches "with his flag between his knees." Yet later he is singled out as a hero, a "jim-hickey" (Chap. 22/21, DD). In the second battle, he now resolves not to budge, and yet we see him in action – not killing the enemy but this time vainly coveting the enemy flag.

Early (Chapters 3–6) the conjoined themes of spectator and spectacle were linked in terms of watching the flag. Now the presentation of the youth as self-confirming spectator suggests that the flag should be read as a figure of bitter irony. The role of color bearer that the youth so desires can be seen as the equivalent of a cheerleader – but, more importantly, it represents the position of one who does not fight. Of course, on the first day the youth does shoot and perhaps kills; but this aspect of his experience is curiously muffled. When he later becomes a "wild-cat," it is as the captor of the enemy flag, and his bravery is thus presented as useless exposure. That posture is twice ridiculed when the lieutenant stands with his "forgotten back" toward the enemy and curses. The youth's plans to *get* killed – first as the only answer to his problem and later as revenge on the general – are part of the same ironically pointless pattern. As was the notion of risk-free heroism the youth attributed to women at the end of Chapter 16. Finally, the idea of the youth redeeming himself as color bearer deconstructs itself. He is said to have been brave again, but we are

not allowed to witness it as spectators, and can only watch him
watching. The rest is the spectacle of the flag bearer, in which
spectator and spectacle have become one.

Courage and cowardice

A narrative endlessly tells the story of its own denominational
aberration.

−Paul de Man

There would seem to be nothing left to say about courage independent of cowardice, since the concepts are so intricately woven into
one another. The fact that Crane thought of his book as a study of
fear adds little to this deadlock, since fear is not a simple opposite
of courage. Courage and cowardice are themselves opposite ways
of dealing with fear. Yet *Red Badge* offers a constant shifting and
reversal of values, both for the youth and the reader, and we need
to attend to the steady buildup toward the culmination of those
reversals in Chapter 18/17. For three quarters of the novel, courage is associated with calculation, curiosity, overly valiant airs, a
death wish, selflessness, membership, battlesleep, an absence of
heroic poses, rage, exasperation, ecstasy, envy, and the expectation of success. Cowardice during this same period is associated
with calculation, fear of ignominy, revelation, crime, shame, and
fear of questioning. Importantly, courage is hardly ever valued
positively or treated other than ironically. The youth's running
away, conversely, is never valued negatively except by himself.

From Chapter 18/17 on, cowardice seemingly disappears, and
yet ordinary reversals now occur between the two concepts. Courage has now become hatred for the foe, for the general, and for the
universe, unconsciousness, determination, a dog game, shooting
alone, beastliness, insanity, frenzy, foolhardiness, patriotism, revenge, stalwartness, despair, and so on to the "red sickness" of the
last page. The only positive evaluation of courage, in a notably
ironic authorial voice, is the statement "There was a delirium that
encounters despair and death. It is a temporary but sublime absence of selfishness" (Chap. 20/19). And one might well ask, what
is the value of courage if it is punished in the irony of event? The
seeming reward for the youth's first bravery is another attack (and

his flight); that for his second (firing for nothing) is to overhear his unit being called mule-drivers; for his third, the mockery of veterans and the general's fury. The colonel's distantly transmitted praise, which itself is not guaranteed for the reader, can hardly be said to compensate.

Soldiers in battle, then, are animals and savages, no better than "a dog, a woman an' a walnut tree" (Chap. 18/17). Moreover, the use of the words "man" and "manhood" as apparent equivalents for courage is highly ironical both at moments of courage and when it seems denied: "He became not a man but a member" (Chap. 5, NS); he feels below "the standard of traditional manhood" but through lies is "returned to his comrades unimpeached" (Chap. 16/15, RT); "He had performed his mistakes in the dark so he was still a man" (Chap. 16/15, RT); or again, "they returned to caution. They were become men again" (Chap. 20/19, NS). Manhood is at other times equated with caution, or with revenge, or even with a deceiving gentleness. Yet the final identification is perhaps most ironic: "He felt a quiet manhood. . . . He had been to touch the great death, and found that, after all, it was but the great death and was for others. He was a man" (Chap. 25/24, RT). The youth's self-ignorant satisfaction, confirmed here in the original clause, "and was for others," thoroughly undercuts his notion of manhood.

Henry Binder has conjectured that the ellipsis at the end of Chapter 15/14 caused by lost manuscript pages must have included a guilty recollection of the youth's desertion of the tattered soldier. His rationale is that "Henry commits three acts that cause him to be ashamed: his flight from battle, his rebellion against nature, and his desertion of the tattered soldier." Since only two of these are recalled in the existing text, the third must have been lost. Yet Binder neglects the youth's other misdeeds precisely because they do not "cause him to be ashamed." Of the three that do, the desertion of the tattered soldier is indeed the most serious; the rebellion against nature, on the other hand, seems trivial and no more than a minor instance of many similar projections by the youth.

By contrast, far more shameful acts are presented than either the flight or the rebellion, which presumably have generated little attention because the youth also represses them. For instance, he lies about his desertion and wound in order to pass himself off as a hero, and then plans to blackmail Wilson with his letters, rejoicing "in the possession of a small weapon with which he could prostrate his comrade" (Chap. 15/14, RT). Both of these acts result from the fear that his flight will be discovered, and although the first deception mildly embarrasses him, the blackmail plan does not. When Wilson's candor prevents it, he even considers his nonaction "a generous thing" and disdains Wilson for his shame at having entrusted his letters to another: "He had never been compelled to blush in such manner for his acts; he was an individual of extraordinary virtues" (Chap. 16/15, RT). Having now forgotten his own shifting furies and humiliations, he is incapable of recognizing the most shameful act of all. He blackmails his loyal friend out of sheer terror at being questioned, much as he had deserted the tattered soldier. Both actions, like the lie about the wound, are part of the "mistakes in the dark" that he thinks enable him to be "still a man." These are merely the means, however, by which the first mistake remains in the dark.

These two straightforward scenes of moral cowardice are embedded in a narrative that everywhere inverts the concepts of physical courage and cowardice. The youth's quiet suppressions, then, compound the irony of events presented throughout with an irony of silence about events. Physical courage? Physical cowardice? The concepts are almost meaningless in battle, where all men become little more than savages. But moral courage and cowardice are oppositions latent under the manifest ones – under the "little red badge of courage" and "the sore red badge of his dishonor." These cannot be inverted or fused precisely because they are not talked of, not turned into legend.

In and out: Fleming and Crane

You must remember that in a battle or a war everything has been prepared which is what has been called begun and then everything happens at once which is called done and then a battle or a war is either not or won.

—Gertrude Stein

143

The author's viewpoint and discourse is clearly outside the youth's and defines him at every turn. Self-revealing as is the youth's RT, it is always controlled and sometimes doubled by the author's irony.[5] The style is thus broadly monological. Yet the very instability of the irony brings it occasionally close to the dialogical. The youth's constant worry about what "they" will think forms a considerable tension in the novel and defines part of the in/out concept that governs all the others. Sometimes the "they" even include the author who defines him:

> He imagined the whole regiment saying: "Where's Henry Fleming? He run, did't 'e? Oh, my! . . . . Wherever he went in camp, he would encounter insolent and lingeringly-cruel stares. As he imagined himself passing near a crowd of comrades, he could hear someone say: "There he goes!" . . . He seemed to hear someone make a humorous remark in a low tone. At it, the others all crowed and cackled. *He was a slang-phrase.* (Chap. 11, emphasis added, RT)

He fears he has become the other's label, or in Bakhtin's terms, the author's "word" on him, and in a canceled passage of Chapter 16, even blames the whole "sniveling race" of poets.

Chapter 11, in particular, fluctuates as he changes attitude, and the suppressed Chapter 12 interestingly continues this faint trace of what Bakhtin terms "the dialogical process." It is reminiscent of a Dostoevskian hero answering and anticipating the word of the other, except that here this imagined word is given; it is not what Bakhtin called the "hidden polemic," which replies to an unstated dialogue. The hidden polemic of *Red Badge* is in fact that which is never said by either author or character. It is instead latent in the very deconstruction of every stable opposition, in the swallowing of each concept by its opposite. The latent polemic is not about running away or lying about it or redeeming oneself or even "growing." It is about the rhetoric of war – the legend, the spectacle, the bullying and galvanizing of men into action. As well, it is about what this does to them by converting them – into either (on the courage side) savages, animals, symbol lovers, unconscious creatures, voyeurs and show-offs, or (on the cowardice side) into self-pitying children, liars, braggarts, and blackmailing sentimentalists. "The red animal, war" not only gobbles men but makes them insignificant when left ungobbled: "And the most startling thing was to learn suddenly that he was very insignificant. The officer spoke of the regiment as if he referred to a broom . . . It was war, no doubt, but it appeared strange" (Chap. 19–18).

All the author's ironies about the youth escape into another irony, shared perhaps with the youth and certainly with us, about war as told and re-created in legend. That story undermines itself in its very failure to denominate, as the constant deconstructions keep shifting the perspective. If the last two paragraphs of *Red Badge* have caused so much critical discussion over the sentimentality of either the author or the character, it is largely because of this final irony – about the way war turns men into either brutes or sentimental lost children. The author, having swallowed the youth into his irony, then spills him out on another less explicit level. In the central chapters (11 and 12) and again in the last two paragraphs, he leaves him free and selfish but still "unfinished," separate to the last, unable, as Bakhtin puts it, to "coincide with himself."

Or so it would seem, right up to the original ending of the novel (at "walking-sticks"). But the three sentences added to the Appleton text enclose him again in one final irony:

> He had rid himself of the red sickness of battle. The sultry nightmare was in the past. He had been an animal blistered and sweating in the heat and pain of war. He turned now with a lover's thirst, to images of tranquil skies, fresh meadows, cool brooks; an existence of soft and eternal peace. (Chap. 25/24, RT)

The youth may feel he has earned this contrast, but clearly he is deluded. For as a pragmatic truth, one local battle does not end a war, and he will go back into the red sickness that, like all sicknesses, lies within.

NOTES

1. Susan Sontag, "The Aesthetics of Silence", in *Styles of Radical Will*, London, Secker, & Warburg, 1969; Roland Barthes, *S/Z*. Paris, Seuil, 1970, transl. Richard Miller, Hill & Wang 1974; Mikhail Bakhtin, *Problems of Dostoevsky's Poetics* (1929), transl. W. Rotsel, Ann Arbor, 1973, new transl. Caryl Emerson, University of Minneapolis Press, 1984.

2. For example, classically: *Emma mit un châle sur ses épaules, ouvrit la fenêtre et s'accouda. La nuit était noire. Quelques gouttes de pluie tombaient* (Flaubert, *Madame Bovary*, cited Ann Banfield, 104). See also her Chap. 5 for examples of unselfconscious perception, particularly when the name of the character is given. *Unspeakable Sentences*, London, Routledge, p. 206.

3. It is fascinating, in this respect, that one of the most aberrant of the Appleton changes was to make the youth alone speak correct English. In the manuscript, the army dialect is not even a matter of rank, and is spoken in more or less unvaried versions by the lieutenant, the colonel, and the general.

4. For instance, the lieutenant's near presence just before he runs (Chap. 6), Wilson's comments about so many returning who had been assumed dead (Chap. 15/14), and the corporal's comments on the youth's wounds (Chap. 14/13) all imply that his comrades are not as unconscious of his flight as he seems to think.

5. For Bakhtin, this type of "outness" is implicitly condemned; the privileged term is "in," though in dialogism it is constantly affected by an imagined outer voice. Bakhtin's examples are always in the first person, in part perhaps because it is technically harder to think dialogically in RT.

Notes on Contributors

Christine Brooke-Rose is Professor of American Literature at the University of Paris at St. Denis. She first achieved prominence with *A Grammar of Metaphor* (1958), and has since published *A ZBC of Ezra Pound* (1971), *A Rhetoric of the Unreal* (1981), and a number of novels and short stories.

Andrew Delbanco, who is Associate Professor of English at Columbia University, is coeditor of *The Puritans in America: A Narrative Anthology* (1985) and author of *William Ellery Channing: An Essay on the Liberal Spirit in America* (1981). He is presently completing a study of the Puritan migration to New England.

Howard C. Horsford, Professor of English and American Literature at the University of Rochester, has published essays on Melville, Hawthorne, Washington Irving and Caroline Gordon, and has recently completed editing Melville's journals.

Amy Kaplan is an Assistant Professor of English and American Studies at Mount Holyoke College who has written on Howells, Wharton, and American realism. She is completing a book on American realism and social change and plans a book on the culture of American imperialism.

Lee Clark Mitchell is Director of American Studies and Associate Professor of English at Princeton University. The author of essays on Adams, Twain, London, and Dreiser, he has published *Witnesses to a Vanishing America: The Nineteenth-Century Response* (1981).

Hershel Parker is H. Fletcher Brown Professor of English at the University of Delaware. A widely published authority on the American Renaissance, he is presently at work on a biography of Melville. His most recent book, on textual problems with Crane, Twain, and Mailer, is entitled *Flawed Texts and Verbal Icons: Literary Authority in American Fiction* (1984).

Selected Bibliography

Albrecht, Robert C. "Content and Style in *The Red Badge of Courage.*" *College English* 27 (March 1966):487–92.

Bergon, Frank. *Stephen Crane's Artistry.* New York: Columbia University Press, 1975.

Berryman, John. "Stephen Crane: *The Red Badge of Courage,*" in *The American Novel: From James Fenimore Cooper to William Faulkner,* ed. Wallace Stegner. New York: Basic Books, 1965, pp. 86–96.

Binder, Henry. "The *Red Badge of Courage* Nobody Knows." *Studies in the Novel* 10 (1978):9–47.

Bowers, Fredson. "The Text: History and Analysis," in Stephen Crane, *The Red Badge of Courage.* C.E.A.A. Text. Charlottesville: University of Virginia Press, 1975, pp. 183–252.

Cady, Edwin H. *Stephen Crane.* New York: Twayne, 1962.

Colvert, James B. "Structure and Theme in Stephen Crane's Fiction." *Modern Fiction Studies* 5 (Autumn 1959):199–208.

Cox, James T. "The Imagery of *The Red Badge of Courage.*" *Modern Fiction Studies* 5 (Autumn 1959):209–19.

Crews, Frederick C. Introduction to *The Red Badge of Courage.* Indianapolis: Bobbs-Merrill, 1964, pp. vii–xxiii.

Dillingham, William B. "Insensibility in *The Red Badge of Courage.*" *College English* 25 (December 1963): 194–8.

Frohock, W. H. "*The Red Badge* and the Limits of Parody." *The Southern Review* 6 (1970):137–48.

Frykstedt, Olov W. "Henry Fleming's Tupenny Fury: Cosmic Pessimism in Stephen Crane's *The Red Badge of Courage.*" *Studies Neophilologica* 33 (1961):265–81.

Gibson, Donald B. *The Fiction of Stephen Crane.* Carbondale: Southern Illinois University Press, 1968.

Greenfield, Stanley B. "The Unmistakable Stephen Crane." *PMLA* 73 (December 1958):562–72.

Griffith, Clark. "Stephen Crane and the Ironic Last Word." *Philological Quarterly* 47 (January 1968):83–91.

Hart, John E. *"The Red Badge of Courage* as Myth and Symbol." *University of Kansas City Review* 19 (Summer 1953):249–56.

Howarth, William L. *"The Red Badge of Courage* Manuscript: New Evidence for a Critical Edition." *Studies in Bibliography* 18 (1965):229–47.

Hungerford, Harold R. " 'That Was at Chancellorsville': The Factual Framework of *The Red Badge of Courage.*" *American Literature* 34 (January 1963):520–31.

Johnson, George W. "Stephen Crane's Metaphor of Decorum." *PMLA* 78 (June 1963):250–6.

Katz, Joseph. "Afterword: Resources for the Study of Stephen Crane," in *Stephen Crane in Transition: Centenary Essays.* Dekalb: Northern Illinois University Press, 1972, pp. 205–31.

Krauth, Leland. "Heroes and Heroics: Stephen Crane's Moral Imperative." *South Dakota Review* 11 (1973):86–93.

LaFrance, Marston. "Stephen Crane's *Private Fleming: His Various Battles,"* in *Patterns of Commitment in American Literature,* ed. Marston La France. Toronto: University of Toronto Press, 1967, pp. 113–33.

Levenson, J. C. Introduction to Stephen Crane, *The Red Badge of Courage.* C.E.A.A. Text. Charlottesville: University of Virginia Press, 1975, pp. xiii–xcii.

Mailloux, Steven. *"The Red Badge of Courage* and Interpretive Conventions: Critical Response to a Maimed Text." *Studies in the Novel* 10 (1978):48–63.

Marcus, Mordecai. "The Unity of *The Red Badge of Courage,"* in *The Red Badge of Courage: Text and Criticism,* ed. Richard Lettis et al. New York: Harcourt, Brace, 1960, pp. 189–95.

Nagel, James. *Stephen Crane and Literary Impressionism.* University Park: Pennsylvania State University Press, 1980.

Overland, Orm. "The Impressionism of Stephen Crane: A Study in Style and Technique," in *Americana Norvegica: Norwegian Contributions to American Studies,* Vol. I. Philadelphia: University of Pennsylvania Press, 1966, pp. 239–85.

Pease, Donald. "Fear, Rage, and the Mistrials of Representation in *The Red Badge of Courage,"* in *American Literary Realism,* ed. Eric Sundquist. Baltimore: Johns Hopkins University Press, 1982, pp. 155–175.

Perosa, Sergio. "Naturalism and Impressionism in Stephen Crane's Fiction," in *Stephen Crane: A Collection of Critical Essays,* ed. Maurice Bassan. Englewood Cliffs, N.J.: Prentice Hall, 1967, pp. 80–94.

Pizer, Donald. *Realism and Naturalism in Nineteenth-Century American Literature.* Carbondale: Southern Illinois University Press, 1966.

"The Red Badge of Courage Nobody Knows: A Brief Rejoinder." *Studies in the Novel* 11 (Spring 1979):77–81.

Schmitz, Neil. "Stephen Crane and the Colloquial Self." *Midwest Quarterly* 14 (1972):437–51.

Solomon, Eric. *Stephen Crane: From Parody to Realism.* Cambridge, Mass.: Harvard University Press, 1967.

Stein, William Bysshe. "Stephen Crane's *Homo Absurdus.*" *Bucknell Review* 8 (May 1959):168–88.

Vanderbilt, Kermit, and Daniel Weiss. "From Rifleman to Flagbearer: Henry Fleming's Separate Peace in *The Red Badge of Courage.*" *Modern Fiction Studies* 11 (Winter (1965–6):371–80.

Walcutt, Charles C. "Stephen Crane: Naturalist and Impressionist," in his *American Literary Naturalism: A Divided Stream.* Minneapolis: University of Minnesota Press, 1956, pp. 66–86.

Weiss, Daniel. "*The Red Badge of Courage.*" *Psychoanalytic Review* 52 (Summer, Fall 1965):32–52, 130–54.

Westbrook, Max. "Stephen Crane's Social Ethic." *American Quarterly* 14 (Winter 1962):587–96.